Design for Hospitality
PLANNING FOR ACCESSIBLE HOTELS & MOTELS

Thomas D. Davies, Jr., AIA
Kim A. Beasley, AIA
Illustrated by the Authors
and Stephan B. Alicandro, AIA

Paralyzed Veterans of America
with assistance from the
American Hotel and Motel Association

NICHOLS PUBLISHING

Manufactured in the United States of America.

Published by Nichols Publishing
155 West 72nd Street
New York, NY 10023
Nichols is an imprint of GP Publishing Inc.
A General Physics Company

LIBRARY OF CONGRESS CATALOGING-IN-PUBLICATION DATA
Davies, Thomas
    Design for hospitality : planning for accessible hotels and motels
  / Thomas Davies and Kim Beasley.
        p.   cm.
    ISBN 0-89397-318-1 : $39.95
    1. Architecture and the physically handicapped--United States.
  2. Hotels, taverns, etc.--United States--Access for the physically
  handicapped. 3. Motels--United States--Access for the physically
  handicapped. I. Davies, Thomas, 1946-   . II. Title.
  NA2545.P5B4 1988
  728' .5' 042--dc19   88-19664
Printed and bound by Semline Corporation   CIP

Acknowledgments

Design for Hospitality was developed by the Paralyzed Veterans of America (PVA) with assistance from the American Hotel and Motel Association (AH&MA). PVA is chartered by the United States Congress as a veterans' service organization whose primary focus is the special needs of thousands of veterans who have a spinal cord injury or disease. Since its inception in 1947, PVA has been a strong advocate for architectural accessibility. PVA acquired the Accessibility Resource Library from the National Center for a Barrier Free Environment (NCBFE) in 1984 when the center ceased operations. The idea for this book and many of the resources used in its writing originated with the NCBFE and are now an important part of PVA's national program to promote barrier free design.

The American Hotel and Motel Association represents the interests of every segment of the lodging industry. Matters pertaining to design and construction of hotel and motel facilities are often addressed by the AH&MA Executive Engineer's Committee (EEC). In 1983, the committee took a proactive stance toward accessible lodging facilities and appointed a special subcommittee to address this subject. The AH&MA EEC subcommittee, together with the NCBFE, developed an interpretation of the *American National Standards for Buildings and Facilities - Providing Accessibility and Usability for Physically Handicapped People* (ANSI A117.1) as applicable to new hotels and motels. The AH&MA EEC subcommittee members have generously contributed their time, talent, and experience to the development of this book: Raymond B. Hambel, Hilton Hotels Corporation, chairman; John P. S. Salmen, American Hotel & Motel Association; James A. DiLuigi, Marriott Corporation; Charles C. Cocotas, Lehr Associates; Scott McLean, Radisson Hotel Corporation; Robert Aulbach, RoBach, Inc.; Digby Brown, Rockresorts, Inc.; Harold Roffman, Affordable Inns, Inc.; Thomas Larsen, Park Lane Hotel International; Edward Dietz, Stoeffer Hotels; and William Smith, Chicago Hilton & Towers.

Sponsors

The following companies have underwritten the direct costs of developing this publication. Each sponsor company has a history of interest in accessible design and manufactures products to aid people with functional impairments. We express our gratitude for their generosity.

The Stanley Works of New Britain, Connecticut has extensive experience in barrier-free design. The company's Magic-Door division engineers, manufactures, and distributes a complete line of door automation products designed to improve accessibility for people with disabilities. In addition to its quality products, The Stanley

Works is nationally recognized for corporate citizenship, including the efforts of Stanley's Public Policy Council. This council is composed of Stanley employees who work in support of programs that seek to improve the quality of life in the communities in which they live.

James J. Scott, P.E., Marketing Manager of Stanley Magic-Door and chairman of the Stanley Public Policy Council Subcommittee on Health and Human Services, contributed to the development of this book.

Aqua Glass Corporation of Adamsville, Tennessee, manufactures one of the most extensive lines of contemporary bath products for the physically impaired. With its Special Care® line, Aqua Glass was the first member of the industry to introduce thermostatic temperature controls and hand-held showers. Aqua Glass is committed to providing products that offer independence and safety for bathers. As one of the country's largest manufacturers of fiberglass bath products, Aqua Glass is an active supporter of the contract work program for its community's physically impaired and developmentally disabled citizens.

Arther Crotts, Director of Marketing Services, Aqua Glass Corporation, contributed his experience in working with persons having physical and cognitive impairments to the development of this book.

AT&T's National Special Needs Center celebrated its fifth anniversary in January, 1988. Created after the breakup of the Bell System to continue AT&T's commitment to disabled consumers, the center is chartered as the central source within AT&T to solve the communications needs of persons with physical disabilities.

The center provides a variety of products aimed at meeting the special communications needs of persons with hearing, speech, vision, or motion impairments. Products include handsets for hearing and speech amplification, signaling devices for hearing-impaired persons, dialing aids for persons with low vision or an artificial larynx, and special telephones for motion-impaired people. Four telecommunications devices for the deaf (known as TDDs) with a wide range of features are also included in the line.

Sue Decker, Manager of Sales Development for the Special Needs Center, contributed to the development of this book.

REVIEWERS

The following organizations have reviewed a partial draft of the material presented in this design guide. We appreciate their time and assistance.

American Association of Retired Persons
American Council of the Blind
American Hotel and Motel Association (EEC)
Association of Retarded Citizens
Multiple Sclerosis Society
National Association of the Deaf
National Easter Seal Society
National Organization on Disability
National Spinal Cord Injury Association
Ohio Governor's Office of Advocacy for People
      with Disabilities
Paralyzed Veterans of America
United Cerebral Palsy Association, Inc.

SPECIAL THANKS

During the development of this book, there were many individuals whose efforts greatly enhanced its quality and timeliness. The desktop publishing and organizational skills of Denise Hannan were indispensable. The careful preparation of the manuscript from beginning to end can be attributed to her. John Salmen, Jim DiLuigi, and Charlie Cocotas of the AH&MA Executive Engineers Committee provided reviews, comments and input throughout the development of each chapter. Their professional insight from a hospitality industry perspective was extremely helpful. Manuscript editing performed by Susan Robbins added polish to the book. Numerous small but important details associated with the final preparation of the manuscript were expertly handled by Kathryn White and Meredith Davies. Many PVA members and national staff offered assistance and encouragement including R. Jack Powell, Gordon Mansfield, Vic McCoy, Al Virellas, Dennis Smurr, Frank DeGeorge, Doug Vollmer, Dave Capozzi, Tom Stripling, Linda Mansfield, Mike Delaney, Charles Karczewski, Skip Drepps, Rick Glotfelty, and Kai Yee. In addition, we thank the management and staff of hotels and motels who shared their experiences, showed us their properties, provided photographs and brochures, and extended to us their hospitality.

Table of Contents

Table of Contents

Hospitality is a tradition of the lodging industry.　(I-1)

Introduction
Hospitality and Accessibility

The hospitality industry can trace its roots to earliest recorded times. The Roman government established the first organized system for lodging with *mansiones,* temporary shelters along their roads to serve government officials traveling in the expanding empire. Spas, constructed by Roman engineers in England and other colonies, were the first resort hotels. In the Middle Ages, abbeys and monasteries offered lodging to travelers. The word *hospice* is derived from an abbey in the Swiss Alps operated by the monks of St. Bernard, who not only offered shelter and hospitality but also bred and trained dogs to rescue lost travelers. Country inns began in England in the 1200s, and 200 years later, the British government established the first regulations for the lodging industry. In colonial America, Massachusetts law reportedly required that every town provide an inn to serve travelers.

Today, lodging facilities offer guests a variety of specialized services. In addition to traditional hotels, motor inns, and resorts, travelers can stay at convention hotels, casino hotels, conference centers, or suite hotels. In every type of facility, a wide range of costs and services is available from budget motor inns to luxurious and expensive resort hotels.

Hospitality – satisfying guests' needs and ensuring that every stay is a pleasant experience – is the service provided by every lodging facility. Successful hospitality results from an understanding and concern for the needs of guests, which are reflected in personal services from staff and the design of the physical environment.

In today's society, many guests have permanent or temporary functional impairments that may require elements of the physical environment be designed to assist them in performing basic activities. Accessible design is therefore the basis for hotels and motels to extend their hospitality. Accessible design also provides an environment that makes activities easier, safer, and more pleasant for every guest. Accessible design is a practical, cost-effective, and enduring alternative, based on functional objectives rather than the more transient qualities associated with design for style or entertainment.

ACCESSIBLE DESIGN

What is accessible design? The term *accessible* is applied to elements of the physical environment that can be approached, entered, and used by people with physical disabilities. Originally, the term *accessible* described buildings or components that could be entered or used by individuals in wheelchairs. The term has slowly expanded and evolved to include design standards for a larger group of people with a wide range of functional impairments. In its broadest sense, accessible design is any design intended to make basic tasks easier and safer for as many people as possible.

Accessible design has evolved slowly. Wounded soldiers returning from France after World War I encountered buildings, parks, and transportation systems with no provisions to serve them. Significant advances in medicine allowed more injured veterans to return from World War II. During the war, the country was led by a president who could not walk without the aid of crutches. Nevertheless, veterans' hospitals designed and constructed in the late 1940s and early 1950s remained inaccessible to patients or visitors in wheelchairs.

Post-war architecture enjoyed new freedom in design due to advances in construction methods, materials, and mechanical systems. These advances, however, were not focused on the needs of people with functional impairments. Designs often responded to the demands of technology, rather than the needs of users. Architecture failed to keep pace with advances in medicine, which were allowing Americans to live longer and enabled more people with disabilities to continue to lead useful and productive lives.

The first standard for accessible design was the American National Standard A117.1, published in 1961. In 1968, the United States government passed the first federal legislation on accessibility, the Architectural Barriers Act. Many codes and standards have since been developed to address the needs of people with physical handicaps.

Accessibility is also a subject of international interest, and governments in many countries have passed similar laws and regulations. Most public buildings in England, even structures over 1000 years old, now have accessible restroom facilities. Private industry, particularly in Switzerland and the United States, has made significant advances in constructing accessible facilities. An official delegation from the People's Republic of China toured the United States in 1987 to study examples of accessible design to develop codes for their own country; codes that may influence the design of 60,000 new hotel rooms in China during the next 10 years.

OPPORTUNITY for HOSPITALITY

Today, there is a growing need and market for accessible design. A U.S. Department of Commerce survey released in 1986, identified 37.3 million Americans who had difficulty performing basic activities of daily living. This represents one out of every five people over the age of 15, many of whom are older citizens. The number of Americans between the ages of 55 and 74 is projected to increase 13 percent by the year 2000, which does not include the baby boom generation that will reach the age of 55 in the year 2002. The 55 to 74 age group comprises 80 percent of the vacation travelers in the United States, and represents 25 percent of the total consumer spending, more than $500 billion. Demographic projections, combined with future advances in medicine and rehabilitation, indicate that more Americans with functional limitations will be traveling and using lodging facilities in the years to come. It is reasonable to anticipate that these guests will not always travel alone, but with friends, family, and business associates.

Other trends may also influence the lodging industry. Increased sensitivity to individual rights as well as new laws and recent legal decisions have extended the right of access to public facilities to many people with functional impairments. Federal law requires government funded meetings to be scheduled in accessible facilities. Many organizations, including professional associations, clubs, and civic groups, are increasingly reluctant to choose facilities that will not accommodate all their members. Information on accessible lodging facilities is also becoming available to consumers. Several groups are currently conducting surveys that will list accessible hotels and motels in the United States, Canada, and worldwide. The American Association for the Advancement of Science, for example, published a guide to help professional associations plan barrier-free meetings.

PRACTICAL BENEFITS

Is it cost-effective to change the design of a lodging facility to benefit, in some cases, only a small number of guests? A practical aspect of accessible design is that most design features help guests with a wide range of functional impairments. Shelving and operating controls mounted at convenient heights assist guests in wheelchairs, older guests with restricted reach or poor balance, and young children. Good lighting helps guests with restricted vision and helps guests with impaired hearing observe lip movement and body gestures. A good acoustic environment assists guests with hearing aids and also allows guests with restricted vision to use audible cues for navigation and orientation. Wide doors and maneuvering clearances not only aid guests in wheelchairs but also those with canes, crutches, and walkers. Most important, accessible features generally make most tasks and activities easier and more pleasant for every guest.

Features of accessible design often help create safer environments. Slips and falls, for example, may be reduced by eliminating vertical obstructions, providing aids to balance, and installing slip-resistant floor finishes. Proper use of color and texture to identify pedestrian crosswalks helps guests with restricted vision and alerts both drivers and pedestrians to the need for caution. Clear routes of travel are important to guests with restricted vision and may help avoid inadvertent collisions for other guests.

Color, texture, and graphics can be used to communicate information. Symbols in floor tile helped identify shops in Ancient Rome.   (I-2)

Accessible design can also make properties easier to operate and maintain. Eliminating vertical obstructions and providing wider doors and clearances make it easier to move luggage carts, service trays, linen carts, and cleaning equipment. Wall-hung fixtures such as water closets, drinking fountains, and toilet partitions increase maneuvering space and also make the property easier to clean and maintain. Ramps and wide restaurant aisles make it easier for staff to service tables.

COSTS

Additional costs for accessible design depend on the type of hotel or motel and the level of accessibility provided. In public spaces, such as lobbies, corridors, restaurants, or meeting rooms, the costs of basic accessibility are rela-

tively low. In part, this is because these spaces are already large and furnishings are typically more elaborate. In guestrooms, the cost varies with the property's standard design. Studies of other building types in the early 1970s by Perkins and Will, Architects, and the Department of Urban Studies of the National League of Cities suggest that additional costs were between .1 percent and .5 percent of total costs for new construction.

Although current codes require higher standards of accessibility, increased standardization has led to reduced costs for products to meet guests' special needs. Competition and increased sales of equipment such as accessible drinking fountains, grab bars, door hardware, and showers has led to a relative decrease in the cost of these items.

PLANNING and DESIGN

Accessible design should not compromise the visual image of a property or require hotels or motels to take on the appearance of hospitals or nursing homes. However, to successfully integrate these features, an accessible environment should be a design objective from the first stage of the planning process. For example, if the finished floor level of a building is set at 5'-0" above grade, an elaborate ramp will be necessary to reach the front door. However, if the floor level is set 6" above grade, only a sloped walk will be needed.

Accessible features can be subtle or highlighted as added touches of hospitality for everyone. For example, a low closet pole is an obvious feature for guests in wheelchairs. An adjustable pole can be raised or lowered to suit any guests. A split closet, with both high and low poles, serves everyone and many guests will find the low pole easier to see and access.

Guests' ability to have some control of their physical environment is important to their comfort and well being. While early efforts at accessible design were often awkward, better information and more experience can enhance a designer's ability to achieve subtle, yet effective, solutions. Functional design can be attractive and most people appreciate design that helps make their activities easier.

The planning and design process is an important factor in the cost and appearance of accessible design features. An accessible environment should be an initial objective in the early stages of planning, understood by all the design professionals involved in project development, including architects, landscape designers, engineers, interior designers, and the consultants for graphics, food service, meeting services, and other specialties, who all contribute to the development of a project.

OBJECTIVES of THIS BOOK

Design standards become legally binding only through adoption into laws. In many instances, recommendations in this book exceed the requirements of current accessibility codes. Implimentation of these recommendations may be limited by practical considerations.

The primary objectives of this book are to increase the awareness of hotel and motel developers and designers to the needs of guests with functional impairments and to encourage construction of facilities that meet those needs. Specifically, this book endeavors to:

- Identify the need for accessible design as an opportunity for increased sales and customer satisfaction

- Provide detailed design information to allow owners and operators to develop accurate cost comparisons

- Provide recommendations and information to help ensure that the accessible features required by building codes meet the desired objectives

- Propose additional accessible features that provide a higher level of hospitality

To pursue these objectives, this book provides both statistical information on the need for accessible design and detailed design information to evaluate specific alternatives to determine their effect on costs, maintenance, operating procedures, and the visual image of properties.

For design professionals, this book describes the needs of guests with functional impairments and identifies ways the physical environment can allow them to be more active and independent. Although specific recommendations are suggested, design professionals are encouraged to adapt, improve, and develop alternative solutions. In providing these extra measures of hospitality, every hotel or motel will be safer and more pleasant for all guests and staff.

This book is intended only to educate and inform the reader. It is not to serve as an industry standard for hotel and motel design. Whenever possible, technical requirements presented herein are consistent with the 1986 American National Standard (ANSI A117.1). This book is not intended to serve as a substitute for the ANSI standard, nor is it an authorized interpretation of the material included in ANSI.

An inn that has provided lodging for more than 400 years. (I-3)

CONTENT and ORGANIZATION

The material in this book is specifically directed to the design of hotels or motels. The recommendations are not equally appropriate for the design of other facilities (housing for older citizens, for example, or hospitals). The needs of guests with different functional impairments are in some instances in conflict. The intent of all design recommendations is to meet the special needs of guests with a range of different types of functional impairments. To provide a basis for developing and evaluating design alternatives, the reasons for design recommendations are stated whenever possible.

This book is organized into nine chapters, as follows:
Chapter 1 presents available statistical data on the number of people in the United States with functional impair-

ments. This information is correlated to age and combined with demographic projections to develop forecasts for future needs and the market for accessible design. In addition, different types of functional impairments are discussed in terms of their effect on the design of the physical environment. General design recommendations are proposed to assist guests with these impairments.

Chapters 2-8 provide detailed recommendations and suggest alternatives for the design of specific functional spaces or elements common to most hotels and motels. At the end of each chapter, a checklist that summarizes this material is provided. Chapters 2-8 are arranged to correlate with the typical sequence of functional spaces guests might encounter from their first arrival at the property.

Chapter 9 is an overview of the information presented in the book with a focus on costs and benefits. Design recommendations are listed to illustrate the range of guests with different functional impairments who may benefit from each specific recommendation. In addition, the scope, the number of accessible elements that should be provided, and costs are addressed in general terms.

Drawings are dimensioned in feet and inches, indicated above or to the left of each dimension line. The figure in parentheses below the dimension line or to the right of each dimension is the approximate metric equivalent in centimeters.

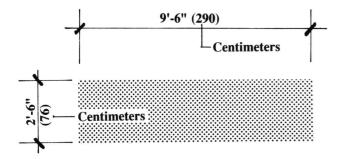

Checklists following each chapter include a list of recommendations that are each preceded by a box that is shaded when the recommendation can be related to a specific ANSI requirement.

Terms associated with accessible design or the hospitality industry can be referenced by use of the index. Lists of photographs and figures, as well as a selected bibliography, follow the appendix.

Guests have a range of needs and capabilities.   (1-1)

Chapter 1
Guests, Challenges and Opportunities

Older travelers and people with functional impairments are active and affluent groups in society and important markets for the lodging industry. To provide comfortable lodging for these guests and a physical environment that supports their activities, developers and designers should understand their needs.

Guests' capabilities can be limited due to a variety of temporary or permanent conditions. Temporary conditions, such as a broken bone, may require a guest to function with one arm in a sling or to use crutches to walk. Showering can impose temporary functional limitations when guests remove eyeglasses. For guests pushing strollers or carrying luggage, a flight of stairs or a narrow door become barriers. Even articles of clothing, such as high heels, can limit guests' abilities to perform certain activities.

The capabilities of some guests are permanently limited as the result of injuries or medical conditions. In addition, many people simply do not meet the design norm in terms of height or weight. Age can also affect guests' capabilities and physical characteristics. Children may not be tall enough to reach a shelf or strong enough to open a door. Older adults commonly experience a decline in strength, stamina, visual acuity, and hearing.

CHALLENGES and OPPORTUNITIES: Advances in medicine and changes in demographics have created a need for buildings and technologies to aid a large and ever-increasing number of people with functional impairments. This user group has increased significantly in this century and is expected to continue to grow. These changes will require new approaches to design and construction of the physical environment.

Design standards are usually based on the user's physical characteristics (weight, height, and reach) and capabilities (strength, vision, or hearing). Such standards are based on the mean, or average, of statistical data. Far more data is available on physical characteristics, than is available on user capabilities. In addition, the majority of data is from records of the armed forces, which may not be completely representative. Very little data is available on older people.

Statistical data is collected over a period of time. Design standards therefore respond slowly to changes in the makeup of society. The planning, design, and construction process is lengthy, and only a relatively small number of new buildings are constructed each year. Therefore, changes in design standards do not result in immediate or significant changes in the total built environment. For many people in today's society, elements of the physical environment can be inconvenient, unsafe, or, in some cases, barriers.

Every design should assist each guest to function as independently as possible, without help from staff or friends. Ideally, each design solution should be suitable for everyone: phones, for instance, mounted at a height appropriate for ambulatory guests, children, and guests in wheel-

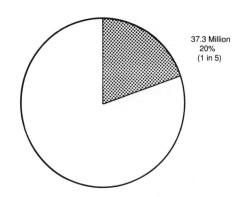

TOTAL POPULATION: 180 Million

37.3 Million
20%
(1 in 5)

Figure 1.10 Americans over the age of 15 with one or more functional impairments represent more than one in every five people.

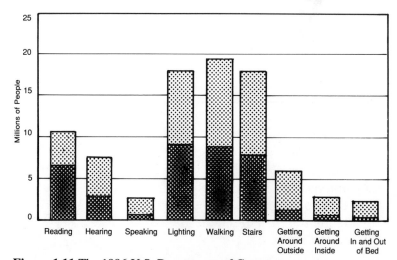

Figure 1.11 The 1986 U.S. Department of Commerce survey identified these basic activities that were sources of difficulty. The hatched area represents people of ages between 15 and 64. The shaded area represents people over 65.

chairs. There are, however, instances in which a single solution does not meet everyone's needs. In these cases, either duplicate facilities or the capacity for adjustment should be provided.

Functional limitations of many Americans were identified in a U.S. Department of Commerce survey released in 1986. The survey indicated that 37.3 million people (one out of every five Americans) over the age of 15 had difficulty performing one or more basic functional activities. Many of these individuals indicated difficulties using sensory information for communication. The study identified 12.8 million persons who reported difficulty seeing letters in ordinary newsprint, even with corrective lenses. Approximately 2.5 million Americans indicated difficulties making their speech understood and over 7.7 million persons identified difficulties hearing normal conversations.

Activities requiring strength and stamina were also identified as problems for many people. Approximately 19.2 million persons indicated they had difficulty walking a quarter of a mile. Over 18 million people had difficulty lifting a bag of groceries, and the same number had difficulty climbing a flight of stairs.

The Commerce Department survey also indicated that mobility and movement were difficult for many Americans. Over 6 million people reported difficulty getting around outside the home, and 3.6 million indicated difficulty in getting around inside the home.

Although the number of individuals in this survey who reported functional limitations is surprisingly high, the results are generally more conservative than those re-

ported in more focused studies. However, regardless of the exact numbers, most of the 37 million people identified by this survey could be assisted by a more accessible physical environment.

Age is a significant factor in the survey results. The Commerce Department Survey indicated almost 22 million people between the ages of 15 and 64 had difficulty performing the basic activities listed above. This represents a surprising 14 percent, or one out of every eight individuals. The survey further indicated that this group included 10 percent of the labor force under the age of 65.

Of the 28 million Americans currently over the age of 65, almost 16 million reported difficulty performing one or more of these basic functional activities. This represents more than 50 percent, or one in every two people. Functional limitations in older people result from the normal aging process and diseases such as arthritis. The capabilities or limitations of specific individuals of any age cannot be predicted. However, the aging process is es-

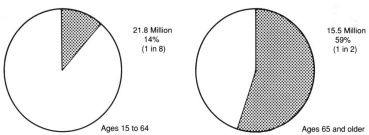

TOTAL POPULATION: 158.5 Million   TOTAL POPULATION: 28 Million

21.8 Million
14%
(1 in 8)

Ages 15 to 64

15.5 Million
59%
(1 in 2)

Ages 65 and older

Figure 1.12 Percentage of Americans with functional limitations within age groups. The probability of individuals over 65 having difficulty performing one of the basic activities is four times greater than in individuals between the ages of 15 and 64.

sentially constant between the ages of 30 and 80. Loss of function for older people is, therefore, not occurring at a more rapid rate but results from the accumulation of more age-related changes. Because of aging and disease, the Commerce Department Survey indicates a four times higher probability that an older person will have one or more functional limitations.

Life expectancy and the average age of our population have changed significantly. While the maximum life span for human beings has remained at approximately 110 years, average life expectancy has increased dramatically in this century. In over 2000 years, average life expectancy slowly increased from 20 years, in Ancient Greece, to 47 years in the United States in the year 1900. However, in the 80 years between 1900 and 1980, life expectancy in the U.S. increased from 47 years to 73 years. This dramatic increase is attributed to many factors, including improved nutrition, higher infant survival rates, and advances in medical care. Simultaneously, new medical procedures, technology, and equipment have also enabled more and more people with disabilities to continue to lead independent and productive lives.

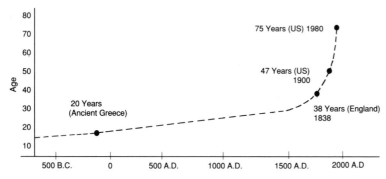

Figure 1.13 During this century the average life expectancy has increased at a dramatic rate.

In 1602, elderly homeless men had to be over the age of 30 to qualify for residency at this almshouse. (1-2)

A demographic shift, unprecedented in history, has resulted from this increase in life expectancy, and is predicted to continue at an accelerated rate in the next 50 years. An increasingly large percentage of our population will be comprised of older citizens. In 1900, only 4 percent of our population was over the age of 65. Today, this group is 13 percent of the total population. By 2040, 22 percent of all Americans will be 65 or older. This is one out of every five people.

Today, there are 62 million consumers in the United States over the age of 50 with a combined annual income of more than $866 billion. This group controls 77 percent of the total financial assets in the country, and one half of the discretionary spending power. Thirty years from now, more than half of the population of the United States will be over the age of 50. This dramatic change will significantly affect every aspect of society. For the lodging industry, it should be evident that the physical environment should respond to the needs of this increasingly large user group.

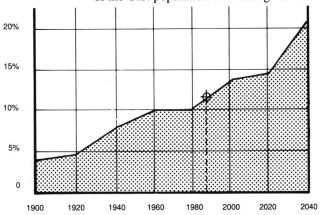

Figure 1.14 The projected growth of the segment of the U.S. population over the age of 65.

DESIGN CONSIDERATIONS: This chapter addresses different types of functional impairments not from a medical perspective, but in terms of their affect on the design of the environment. The organization of these impairments into distinct categories is convenient but could be somewhat misleading. Many people have more than one functional impairment and many functional impairments have secondary effects. For example, low vision can significantly affect a guest's mobility and balance. Because of restricted mobility, a guest may need more strength or stamina to perform a specific task. Poor balance can affect a guest's range-of-motion. Thus, design features intended to assist guests with one functional impairment may often be a secondary benefit to a guest with other functional impairments.

The following general design considerations are very important to most guests with functional impairments:

- **Security**: Guests with functional impairments may be particularly vulnerable to crime or violence. It is important to provide good security measures such as indoor and outdoor lighting, controlled access to buildings and outdoor spaces, guestroom lock systems, and whenever possible, direct staff supervision or television monitors.

- **Temperature Regulation**: Because of a variety of medical conditions, many guests can be sensitive to temperature extremes and excessive heat or cold may cause certain medical problems. Designs should minimize infiltration at windows and doors and provide supplemental heat in areas that may be subjected to continuous cold drafts, such as bathrooms with exterior walls. Room temperatures should be regulated by the guest whenever practical.

- **Independence**: For guests with functional limitations, control of the physical environment is important for self-esteem and self-confidence. Therefore, designs should always allow guests to function as independently as possible, without additional help or special assistance.

- **Safety**: For many guests, evacuation in emergency situations can be difficult. Egress is a particular problem in multistory buildings because of stairs and travel distances. When permitted by codes, fire separations are recommended to create areas of refuge.

Communication through sign language   (1-3)

HEARING: Hearing impairment, ranging from a slight loss of hearing in specific frequency ranges to profound deafness, affects more than 23 million persons in the United States. Many of these individuals are hard-of-hearing, (hearing is restricted) but generally functional for most daily living activities with the help of a hearing aid. With deafness, sounds have no meaning in ordinary living. There are an estimated 2 million profoundly deaf individuals in the United States.

Hearing aids are the most common assistive device for people with impaired hearing, but these devices can only amplify sound and do not enhance clarity. Hearing aids are most effective when the user is face-to-face with the speaker, but are less useful in large groups of people, rooms with high levels of background noise, rooms in which sound reverberates, and situations in which the speaker or sound source is distant from the listener. High-

or low-frequency sounds and static electricity can interfere with hearing aid performance.

When hearing is impaired, there is an increased dependence on other sensory information, particularly visual information. For guests who are deaf, oral or auditory information can be communicated visually through speech-reading or lip-reading, sign language, or finger spelling.

Assistive devices should be available to guests with hearing impairments, including signaling devices that use light or vibration for emergency alarms, doorbells, or wake-up alarms. Listening systems can be used in auditoriums or conference rooms, and closed-caption decoders can be used with televisions. Telephone handset amplifiers should be available for guests who are hard-of-hearing and TDDs (telecommunication devices for the deaf) that can be used with conventional telephones for nonauditory communication.

Guests with impaired hearing can be assisted by:
- Acoustic environments that minimize interference, background noise, and reverberation

- Displays, signals, and warning systems that communicate information in visual as well as audible form

- Assistive devices such as TDDs, closed-captioned decoders, telephone amplifiers, and listening systems

- Lighting to aid communication through speech-reading, sign language, gestures, and body movements

- Counters and furniture groupings configured to allow close face-to-face communication

A long cane is used to negotiate a walk. (1-4)

VISION: Over 6.4 million persons in the United States have restricted vision, which makes seeing and reading difficult, even with corrective lenses. Restrictions to vision result from a number of medical conditions, each of which affects vision in different ways. Guests can experience loss of visual acuity, reduced color discrimination, loss of night vision, tunnel vision, clouding, distortion, or poor vision in conditions with bright light or glare. Over 1.7 million people are legally blind, with very little sight or unable to see at all. Blindness, and even low vision, can affect mobility.

To travel, guests who are blind use canes, guide dogs, or sighted guides. Long canes are used in two ways: the touch technique (the cane is moved from side to side, touching the floor surface 6" to 8" outside each shoulder) or the diagonal technique (the cane is held stationary with

the tip just above the ground outside one shoulder and the grip outside the other shoulder). The touch technique is generally used in unfamiliar or less structured environments, such as sidewalks or parking lots. The diagonal technique is typically used in more familiar or controlled environments, such as lobbies or corridors.

Guide dogs are less commonly used because of the care required and their limitations in many environments. Some blind guests use sighted guides and seldom travel independently. Many individuals with low vision travel without canes or guides.

Nonvisual senses are important to guests with restricted vision. Sounds from automobiles, automatic doors, and telephones, for example, can provide important clues to location. Smells from a restaurant can aid in orientation and a temperature change or draft can often indicate the location of doors or windows. Tactile patterns can be used for guidance and warnings. Most people who are blind perceive some variation in light and are able to discriminate between shadow and sunlight and night and day.

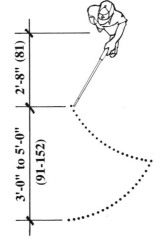

2'-8" (81)

3'-0" to 5'-0" (91-152)

Figure 1.15 With the touch technique, the cane moves side-to-side, touching the ground or floor surface approximately 6" outside the shoulders.

For guests who are blind, negotiating a corridor is part of a larger problem. Other difficulties include orientation and cognitive mapping (developing a mental image of the environment). These tasks are easier in simple and clearly organized indoor or outdoor spaces that provide cues to provide information about location and direction.

Guests with restricted vision and guests who are blind can be assisted by:

- A simple organization of circulation routes and corridor systems to make cognitive mapping easier

- Circulation routes free of obstacles and obstructions that may not be detected by guests using long canes

- Visual and tactile cues, using color and textures to define routes, edges, and interfaces

- Aids to balance such as grab bars and handrails

- Acoustic environments that enhance auditory information and minimize ambient noise

- Uniform general illumination with higher levels of task lighting, diffused and aimed to reduce glare

- Overhangs, louvers, blinds, shades, and sheer curtains to reduce glare from natural light

- Signage with large clear lettering and graphic symbols on contrasting backgrounds, displayed so readers can move closer or further away, as necessary

- Visual information and signals that are also communicated in audible and tactile form

Figure 1.16 Guests with Seeing Eye dogs require additional width at openings and walks.

2'-6" (76) 4'-0" (122)

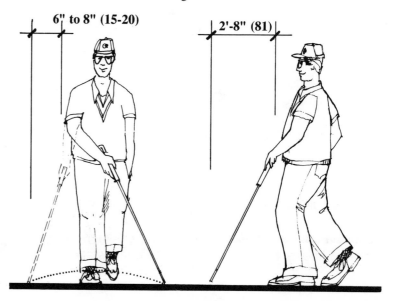

Figure 1.17 Guests who use the long-cane technique may not detect obstacles that overhang or cantilever.

6" to 8" (15-20) 2'-8" (81)

TACTILE SENSES: The partial or total loss of tactile sensory information, such as touch and temperature, is usually present after a stroke, temporary motor loss, or paralysis. Tactile sensitivity also declines with age, as skin becomes drier and less elastic. For these guests, there may be a danger of injury because of their inability to sense contact with sources of heat or abrasion.

Guests with restricted tactile senses can be assisted by:

• Insulation to protect exposed sources of heat that can be inadvertently contacted

• Wall finishes that are not abrasive and furnishings and equipment with smooth rounded edges

• Hot water temperature at sinks, showers, and tubs that is limited to 120 degrees F

Equipment can offer guests a choice of vertical-heights. (1-5)

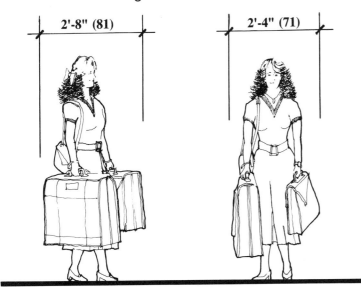

2'-8" (81)   2'-4" (71)

Figure 1.18 Guests carrying suitcases require wider openings and corridors. Stairs or steps also make travel more difficult.

RANGE-OF-MOTION: Many individuals have a limited range-of-motion or a lack of strength in the upper-extremities that restrict lifting, reaching, kneeling, squatting, or bending. A 1970 survey indicated that over 12 million Americans had difficulty lifting or reaching with their arms and 10 million people had difficulty bending, kneeling, or sitting. These conditions can result from injuries, arthritis, heart conditions, inner ear and balance problems, or prosthetic devices.

Vertical- and horizontal-reach can also be a problem for guests who are not "average" in stature. Short guests and children cannot reach as high as taller guests. The average height of a woman over 65 years of age is 5'-1", and her vertical reach is limited to 5'-7", more than 9" lower than a younger male adult. Conversely, tall guests can not conveniently reach as low without bending at the waist or kneeling.

Figure 1.19 The range-of-motion of guests is determined by their anthropometric measurements and their ability to bend, kneel, lean, or stretch. A vertical zone between 2'-3" and 4'-6" and a maximum horizontal-reach of 2'-0" are recommended for the comfort of most guests.

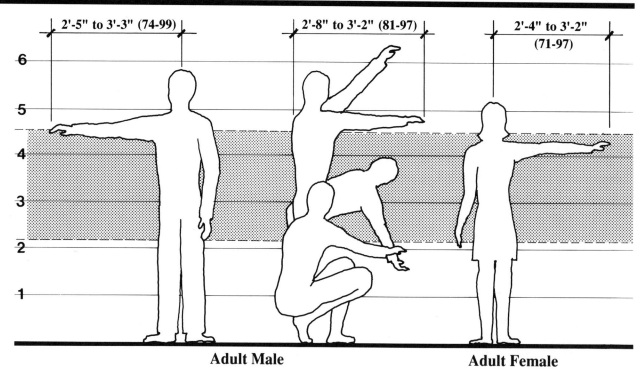

2'-5" to 3'-3" (74-99)   2'-8" to 3'-2" (81-97)   2'-4" to 3'-2" (71-97)

Adult Male   **Adult Female**

Anthropometrics, measurements of the human body, are one basis for design standards related to comfortable range-of-motion. Body measurements vary significantly and are affected by many complex factors, such as age, sex, and race. Design standards are commonly established to serve 90 percent of the user population. Based on a numerical ranking of statistical data, most standards serve users from the 5th percentile to the 95th percentile. Standards are developed on a worst-case basis. For example, the widest requirement (95th percentile) determines the minimum width. In some instances, small adjustments can be made to include a greater percentage of users without sacrifice to the larger user group. In other instances, a specific activity requires a range of alternatives to meet different users' needs or the capacity for adjustment.

Motion or movement is also a factor affecting the ability to perform certain activities. The ability to bend, lean, kneel, or reach is partially a function of the hinge points of the body, such as the knee and elbow. Studies indicate that a number of factors, including weight and sex, affect the range of joint movement. Age, without complicating medical factors, does not significantly reduce (10 percent) the range of joint motion.

Age can affect guests' capabilities to perform certain activities, however. Studies indicate that older people, as a group, are shorter and have a shorter reach. This is partially the result of the generation they represent, since average body size and stature have increased significantly since 1920. Many older people also have difficulty bending or kneeling because of stiff joints, arthritis, or dizziness

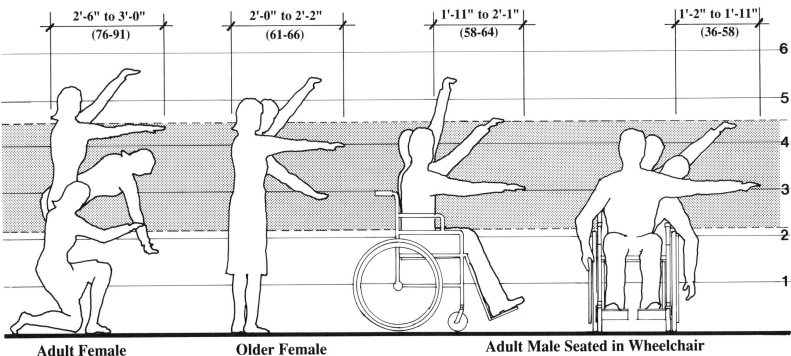

2'-6" to 3'-0"
(76-91)

2'-0" to 2'-2"
(61-66)

1'-11" to 2'-1"
(58-64)

1'-2" to 1'-11"
(36-58)

Adult Female   **Older Female**   **Adult Male Seated in Wheelchair**

associated with inner-ear problems. Impaired balance can also make high vertical-reach difficult.

A guest's range-of-motion can also be restricted by prosthetic devices such as casts or leg braces. Guests in wheelchairs must perform activities from the seated-position, which greatly reduces their range-of-motion. Similarly, ambulatory guests who must maintain balance with assistive devices such as crutches or walkers have difficulty with a low or high vertical-reach.

Guests with a limited range-of-motion can be assisted by:

- Switches, controls, shelving, drawers and other equipment and furnishings mounted at convenient vertical

heights. A range between 2'-3" and 4'-6" above the floor is recommended

- Shelving, desktops, vanities, and countertops that do not require a horizontal-reach greater than 2'-0"

- A choice of alternative heights or the capability of adjusting equipment for the convenience of guests whose stature or weight does not fall within the design user group

- Aids to balance, such as grab bars and handrails, and chairs with armrests to aid in sitting and rising

- Signage and informational displays near eye level to avoid vertigo or balance problems

STRENGTH and STAMINA: Over 5 million Americans have limited stamina or strength to perform daily living activities as a result of a stroke or cardiac condition, hypertension, asthma, emphysema or other breathing problems, spinal cord injuries, multiple sclerosis, or advancing age.

Guests with limited strength or stamina can be assisted by:

- Mechanical aids, such as elevators and automatic doors, to minimize exertion

- Short travel distances between guest activities with periodic rest areas on the routes

- Doors, windows, and furnishings that are light in weight and easy to operate

- Seating at locations where guests may be required to wait for services or meet with friends

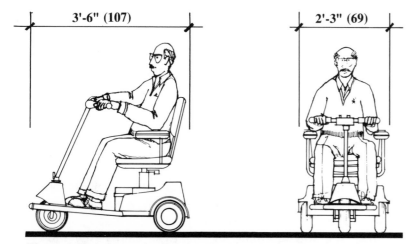

Figure 1.20 A three-wheeled electric wheelchair assists guests with restricted mobility or limited stamina.

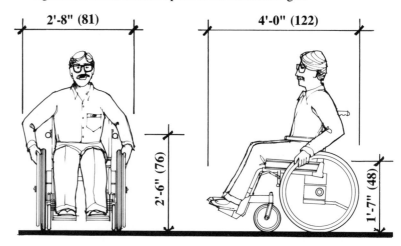

Figure 1.21 Wheelchairs are available in many sizes and designs. A significant factor in knee space is the armrest height.

MOBILITY: More than half a million individuals in the United States use wheelchairs for mobility, and over 7 million persons rely on some form of walking aid for ambulation. Mobility can be restricted due to paralysis resulting from spinal cord injuries, amputation of lower limbs, arthritis, polio, multiple sclerosis, or injuries to the legs or feet. For these individuals, a number of assistive devices are available, including wheelchairs, leg braces, crutches, canes, prostheses, and walkers.

Spinal cord injuries interrupt the nervous system, affecting sensory, motor, and autonomic function below the level of the injury. If only the lower body and legs are affected, the injury is described as paraplegia. If function in the arms and fingers is also affected, the injury is quadriplegia. Other areas that can be affected include bowel and bladder function, tactile senses, fine hand control, forearm muscles, and breathing.

Figure 1.22 Crutches are angled away from the body for greater stability. This requires wider openings and corridors.

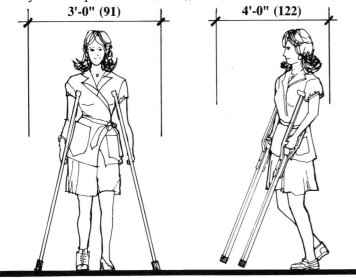

3'-0" (91)   4'-0" (122)

The age and physical condition of the individual and the location and severity of the spinal cord injury determine a guest's functional capabilities. Amputees also use wheelchairs but may have normal function in other areas.

Individuals in wheelchairs represent the full range of anthropometric characteristics in terms of height, weight, and reach. Thus, capabilities and needs vary greatly among individual guests using wheelchairs.

Guests in wheelchairs have a different range-of-movement than most standing ambulatory guests. High-vertical reach is restricted, because a seated position must be maintained. Low reach is more awkward, because the wheelchair must be maneuvered directly above the objective. Horizontal reach is usually easier to the side, because without a kneespace, the footrests restrict forward-reach. Eye level in a seated-position is more than 12 inches lower than that of most standing adults.

To move the body from a wheelchair to a bed, chair, water closet, or tub, guests must execute a transfer. This requires clear space adjacent to the furniture or fixture, and for some transfers, grab bars. Operating equipment that requires excessive force can also be a problem, not because guests lack upper body strength but because of the stability of the wheelchair.

For a front-approach to desks, sinks, tables, or countertops, adequate kneespace must be available below the fixture or furnishing. Wheelchairs require generous clear areas to turn, rotate, and maneuver. Doors and openings must be wide enough to permit passage.

Wheelchairs are available in many models and sizes with a variety of accessories. In the United States, the most common wheelchairs are made of aluminum tubing, with large rear drive-wheels and small front caster-wheels. The frame of the chair is usually collapsible in the middle for storage and transport. Footrests and armrests are generally removable or hinged to swing to the side. Most wheelchairs are propelled with handrims on the rear wheels.

Motorized wheelchairs are driven by electric motors powered by storage batteries below the seat. Movement, either side-to-side or forward and backward, is controlled by a joystick mounted on the armrest. Most motorized wheelchairs are approximately the same size as manual chairs but are heavier and less maneuverable. Three-wheeled electric wheelchairs, which are steered like a bicycle, with a single front wheel are also available. Maneuvering clearances are similar to conventional chairs.

Wheelchairs with large front-drive wheels and small rear caster-wheels are popular in Europe. These chairs are more maneuverable, but the large front wheels restrict access to desks or counters and are often less suitable for outdoor use.

Canes are assistive aids used to reduce stress on leg muscles and joints by shifting a portion of the weight to the arm and shoulder. When additional support or stability is necessary, the small tip (1 1/8" diameter) is replaced by a shoe with three or four points of contact with the ground. Stairs can be a particular problem for guests with canes, and handrails are important to maintain balance. Because injuries can be to either leg, it is important that handrails be available on both sides of all steps and stairs.

Crutches also reduce the stress of weight bearing on the lower extremities. Crutches are either auxiliary (with an underarm-piece to transmit forces to the shoulder) or nonauxiliary (distributing weight to the forearm). Lostrand or Canadian crutches are common types of nonauxiliary crutches. All crutches require good balance skills for ambulation and for performing hand functions (such as operating a door knob) while maintaining a standing position. For stability, crutches are angled away from the body, requiring additional width at doors and openings. If walks or corridors are too narrow, crutches can be a hazard to other pedestrians.

Walkers are also used to decrease stress on joints and muscles and as aids to balance. Walkers are often large and cumbersome, but broader walkers are more stable. Walkers also require wider doors and openings and additional maneuvering room in confined spaces. Walkers are easier to use with ramps, low thresholds, and flush-transitions.

Figure 1.23 Walkers are used to decrease stress in joints and aid balance, but more space is required to maneuver in confined areas.

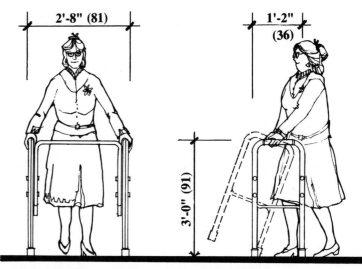

Figure 1.24 Guests with strollers also benefit from ramps, curb-ramps, wider doors, and maneuvering clearances.

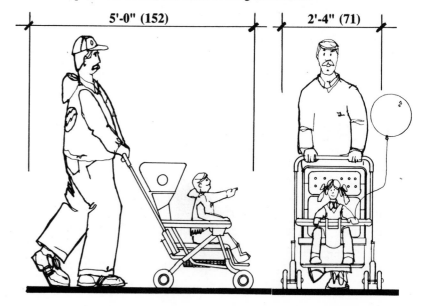

Guests with restricted mobility can be assisted by:

- Doors, openings, and corridors with maneuvering clearances for assistive devices

- Ramps, elevators, lifts, and other alternatives to stairs

- An arrangement of functional spaces that limits travel distances between guest activities

- Automated systems and equipment that do not require rapid movement or agility on the part of users

- Aids to balance and wheelchair transfer, such as handrails and grab bars

- Controls within convenient vertical and horizontal reach of guests with wheelchairs or assistive devices

- Controls and switches that do not require fine hand control or a strong grip to operate

HAND FUNCTION: Over 3 million Americans have difficulty in handling, fingering, grasping, or twisting because of injuries, amputation, stroke, arthritis, or spinal cord injuries.

Guests with limited hand function can be assisted by:

- Furniture and controls that can be operated with one hand rather than both hands

- Operating mechanisms that do not require fine hand control or strong grips and furniture pulls and door hardware that is easily hooked

COGNITIVE ABILITIES: There are many conditions that result in impaired cognitive abilities. Mental retardation is the most common, affecting an estimated 6 million people in the United States. Most of these individuals have mild retardation (IQ 51-70). In addition to cognitive difficulties, people with mental retardation are statistically more likely to also have physical disabilities. Cognitive impairment, particularly for older people, can also result from organic disfunction or Alzheimer's disease.

Guests with impaired cognitive abilities can be assisted by:

- Simple and clearly organized circulation systems with cues (other than written signs) for orientation such as symbols, colors, and identifiable spatial characteristics

- Environments that are not confusing or intimidating

- Environments free from visual misdirection or illusion such as mirrored passageways or invisible railings

- Designs that do not require guests to simultaneously perform multiple activities, such as opening a door while climbing a step, or perform activities in rapid succession, such as a series of closely spaced doors

*   *   *   *

Small modifications to conventional designs can greatly assist all these guests and make their lodging a more pleasant experience. The following chapters address recommended design details for specific functional areas common to most hotels and motels.

Chapter 2
Site Access

Hospitality begins at the point guests first enter the property. (2-1)

An important requirement in the ANSI standard is an accessible route, which is defined as "*a continuous unobstructed path connecting all accessible elements, which can be negotiated by a person with a severe disability using a wheelchair and is also safe for and usable by people with other disabilities*." Requirements for accessible routes are described in terms of minimum widths, heights, and clearances and accessible components such as doors, ramps, stairs, and elevators. The accessible route for hotels and motels should begin outside the walls of the building, at the point where guests and visitors first enter the site.

The site plan for a rural single-story motel is very different from that for a downtown convention hotel. At either facility, however, guests should be able to drive to the property, park, unload, and enter the lobby. To meet these objectives, facilities should have accessible passenger loading zones, accessible parking spaces, and a system of accessible walks, or an elevator to connect these elements to the registration lobby. If public transportation services the site, an accessible route between the transport system and the entrance should be provided.

Outdoor areas and site amenities should be designed for use by guests with functional impairments and connected to building entrances by accessible routes. (See Chapter 7: Recreational Facilities.)

Canopies protect passenger loading zones at major entrances.   (2-2)

PROPERTY ENTRANCE: Access to a property by auto-mobiles, vans, or public transportation is important for guests with many types of functional impairments but particularly guests with restricted mobility. Vehicular and pedestrian entrances to the site should be clearly marked, and directional signs should indicate routes to the registration lobby, guest parking, and secondary entrances such as meeting facilities or restaurants. At urban sites, an accessible walk should connect public sidewalks to hotel and motel entrances so pedestrians are not required to walk in driveways.

PASSENGER LOADING ZONES: Accessible entrances for guests or staff should have passenger loading zones. These protected zones provide vehicular access near building entrances and allow guests to be picked up and discharged safely. All passenger loading zones should in-clude access aisles, curb-ramps, and lighting. Major entrances, such as the registration lobby, should also include canopies.

A canopy, overhang, or porte-cochere is important for guests with functional impairments that restrict mobility. The additional time required to set up assistive devices and unload luggage greatly increases their exposure to in-clement weather. Snow, ice, or even rain on walks and drives can make travel more difficult and hazardous. The route between the canopy and building entrance should also be protected.

Lighting, for safety and security at night, is recommended at all passenger loading zones. The passenger loading zone at the registration lobby and other major entrances should have a lighting level of at least 6 footcandles to aid loading and unloading. Large canopies should include skylights to increase natural lighting during daytime. For waiting, benches, also protected by the canopy, should be provided.

Access aisles at passenger loading zones provide guests with a safe area in which to leave the vehicle and travel to the entrance. ANSI requires access aisles to have a slope less than 1:20, and a minimum width of 4'-0". Access aisles should connect to sidewalks with curb-ramps or flush-transitions.

Access aisles with a width of at least 8'-6" are recom-mended at major entrances. This provides additional space for guests to rotate wheelchairs or exit from lift-equipped vans or buses. (See pages 27 and 28.) Wider aisles can be provided with flush-transitions.

A wide flush-transition with differentiated edges   (2-3)

Lift-equipped vans aid many guests with wheelchairs. Three types of lifts are used by these guests to exit the van: rear platform lifts, side rotary lifts, and side platform lifts. Rear platform lifts lower users from the rear doors and require an 8'-6"-long clear space behind the van. Side rotary lifts lower users vertically onto the driveway, facing parallel to the van. These lifts require a 4'-0" side-aisle and 3'-0" of additional width for access to the controls. Side platform lifts require an 8'-6" wide clear area at the passenger side of the van. Side lifts are also used on many accessible buses.

Any type of lift can exit directly to sidewalks or access aisles on driveways. The additional width required for side platform lifts affects the width of access aisles at passenger loading zones and the raised top on most vans affects the height of canopies.

Flush-transitions, rather than narrow curb-ramps, are also recommended at major entrances. At busy entrances, curb-ramps can be blocked by parked vehicles and can interfere with pedestrians using the adjoining sidewalk. Besides serving guests with restricted mobility, flush-transitions are helpful for strollers, luggage carts, dollies, and suitcases with wheels. At any loading zone, a wide flush-transition helps ensure that passengers with wheelchairs (or other assistive devices) will not be denied access to curb-ramps by the vehicle that discharges them.

At flush-transitions, a contrasting color and/or a change in paving materials should separate vehicular and pedestrian traffic. Bollards, planters, or similar site elements can also help maintain separation. The curbs at both ends of flush-transitions should be painted a bright color to highlight the low, tapered area of the curb, which may trip pedestrians.

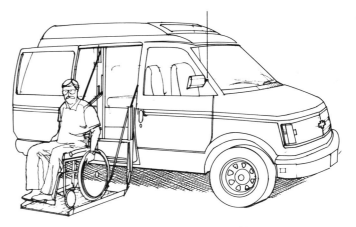

Figure 2.10 Side platform lifts require the widest access aisle. Although the lift can bridge to a sidewalk, the van must be close to the curb to allow the driver to reach the controls to retract the platform.

27

Many vans have raised tops to permit drivers in wheelchairs to move about inside the passenger compartment. Raised tops typically increase the total height of standard vans 12" to 24". With a 24" top, these vans stand 8'-10" above the ground; only 2" below the 9'-0" minimum clearance required for canopies. A minimum canopy height of 9'-6" is therefore recommended.

The entrance to a covered passenger loading zone   (2-4)

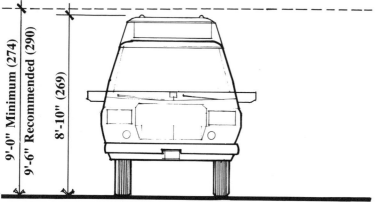

Figure 2.11 Canopies should be a minimum of 9'-0" above the driveway. (9'-6" recommended.)

Figure 2.12 Three types of lifts are available to allow guests in wheelchairs to enter and exit modified vans. Each lift requires different clearances at parking spaces and passenger loading zones. For each lift, the access aisle should include a clear path to the operating controls, usually located in the passenger-side rear quarter-panel.

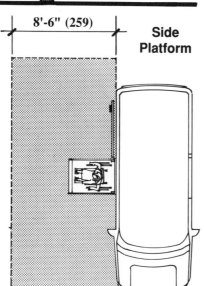

8'-6" (259)   **Side Platform**

6'-0" (183)   **Side Rotary**

8'-6" (259)   **Rear Platform**

Accessible parking designated with post-mounted signs   (2-5)

sible space should be identified and reserved by post-mounted signs at least 3'-0" above grade, so they are not obscured by snow or parked cars.

The location of accessible spaces should allow direct connections to walks so that guests are not required to travel on driveways (between parked cars) to reach the entrance. This is particularly dangerous for guests in wheelchairs, who may not be readily visible to other drivers. Curb-ramps should be provided at each access aisle to connect parking spaces to walks. Where fire lanes require accessible parking to be located across a driveway from entrances, a safe and direct route with crosswalks and curb-ramps should be provided. Outdoor lighting (minimum 1 footcandle recommended) should be provided at accessible parking and along the route to the entrance for nighttime safety.

PARKING: Accessible spaces should provide head-on parking near building entrances to minimize travel distances and exposure to inclement weather. Accessible parking should typically be provided near the entrances to the registation lobby and facilities such as restaurants, lounges, or meeting rooms. At motor inns, parking should also be provided in front of accessible guestrooms.

Accessible parking spaces should have a minimum width of 13'-0"; 8'-0" for the vehicle and a 5'-0"-wide access aisle. Access aisles allow guests to exit and enter vehicles with an assistive device, such as a wheelchair, and travel to the sidewalk or entrance. Adjoining accessible parking spaces may share a common access aisle. The slope of access aisles should not exceed 1:20. Applied-markings or a change in paving materials are recommended to clearly identify the access aisle. Each acces-

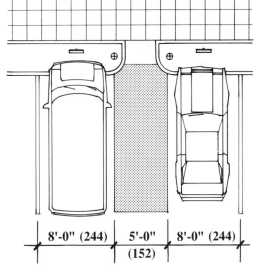

Figure 2.13 Accessible spaces should have a 5'-0" clear aisle beside the vehicle. Adjoining accessible spaces may share a common access aisle. A change in paving materials or applied markings are recommended to identify the access aisle.

8'-0" (244)   5'-0" (152)   8'-0" (244)

29

Figure 2.14 If possible, accessible parking should connect directly to a walk to the main entrance. Where fire lanes require parking to be located across a drive, curb-ramps and crosswalks should be provided. At crosswalks, landscaping should not restrict visibility for children or guests in wheelchairs (eye level, 3'-6"). Lighting can also be used to highlight crosswalks at night. The parking space at the lower left of the plan adjoins a wide walk to accommodate vans equipped with side platform lifts.

Accessible Parking

Crosswalk

Parking for Side-Lift Van   **Accessible Parking**

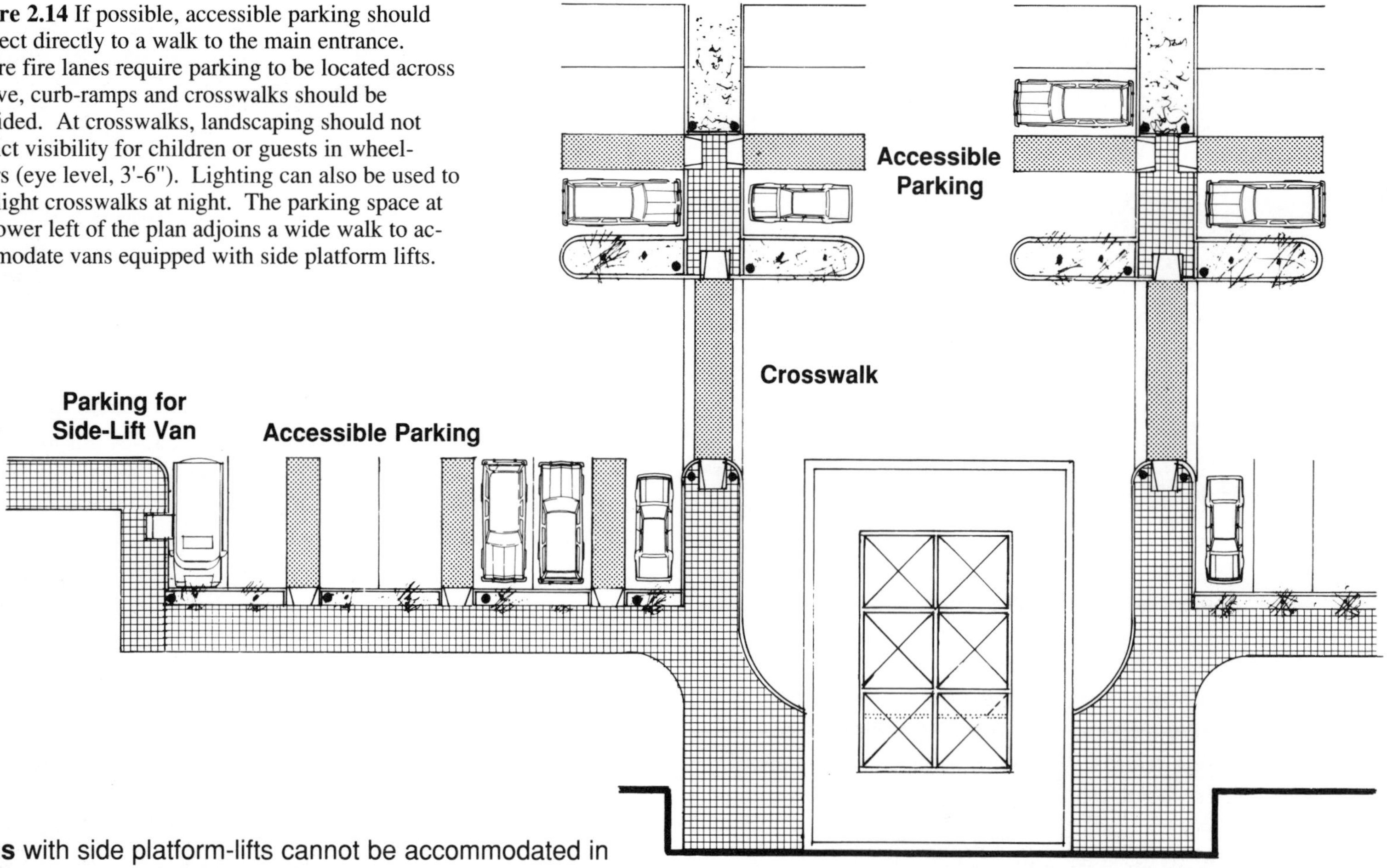

Vans with side platform-lifts cannot be accommodated in conventional accessible parking spaces. These vans require an 8'-6" side clearance and clear access to operating controls to retract the platform and lock the vehicle. Controls are typically located on the passenger-side of the van, above the taillight. This requires extra-wide parking spaces (16'-6") or a wide sidewalk (8'-6") parallel to the parking space. Parking spaces for vans should be reserved, either on grade or within parking structures.

Valet parking for modified vans can also be a problem. Some modified vans cannot be valet parked because attendants cannot operate the hand controls. If on-grade parking is not available, accessible parking spaces should be provided within the parking structure near the elevator lobby. This requires a 9'-0" minimum vertical-clearance at the entrance and at least one parking level.

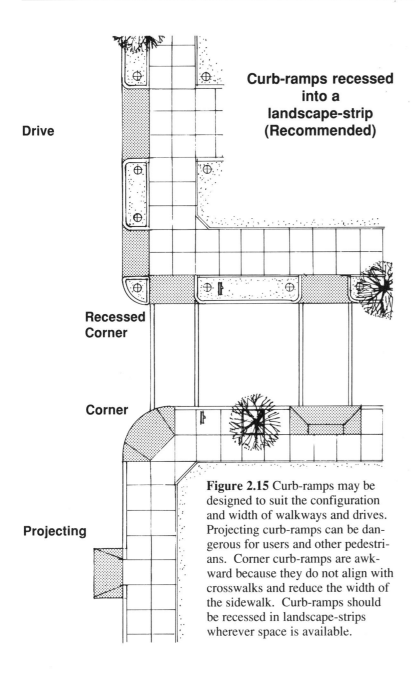

Curb-ramps recessed into a landscape-strip (Recommended)

Drive

Recessed Corner

Corner

Projecting

Figure 2.15 Curb-ramps may be designed to suit the configuration and width of walkways and drives. Projecting curb-ramps can be dangerous for users and other pedestrians. Corner curb-ramps are awkward because they do not align with crosswalks and reduce the width of the sidewalk. Curb-ramps should be recessed in landscape-strips wherever space is available.

Crosswalk with lights and a change in paving material (2-6)

CURB-RAMPS and DRIVES: For guests with wheelchairs or other assistive devices, curb-ramps are essential for reaching walks and entrances from driveways and parking spaces. Curb-ramps should have a minimum width of 3'-0", excluding flared-sides, and a maximum slope of 1:12. This slope is permitted without handrails as a special exception for curb-ramps. The maximum slope for flared-sides is 1:10, and the counterslope, at the gutter for the drive, is limited to 1:20. Curb-ramps should be designed to suit the configuration and width of walkways and drives, as illustrated in Figure 2.15. Curb-ramps should not be located where parked cars can obstruct access.

At driveways, crosswalks and curb-ramps should be provided. Crosswalks can be defined tactilely by a change in paving materials. For safety at night, lighting should identify crosswalks, curb-ramps, and driveway entrances. Low curbs (4" to 6" high) are recommended to reduce the length of curb-ramps and provide a lower step for pedestrians at drives. Landscape-strips between walks and driveways permit curb-ramps to be recessed, increase separation between pedestrians and automobile traffic, and provide space for site elements such as lights and signs.

An urban site with crosswalks and curb-ramps   (2-7)

WALKS: Walks provide pedestrians with access to entrances from passenger loading zones and parking spaces, and may also connect outdoor activity areas (e.g., pools, gardens, and patios) to secondary entrances. The arrangement of accessible elements and the overall walk system should provide the shortest and most convenient routes possible to minimize travel distances.

Walks that serve as accessible routes should be at least 3'-0" wide. A width of 5'-0" is necessary for simultaneous passage of two guests in wheelchairs, and a minimum width of 6'-0" is recommended. Walks less than 5'-0" wide should provide paved areas at convenient intervals to allow guests to wait to pass. Where head-on parking without wheel-stops directly adjoins walks, the width of the walk should allow for 3'-0" of overhang by parked cars.

Materials for walks should provide a firm surface that is reasonably smooth and slip-resistant. Bricks, concrete pavers, or concrete aggregate are all suitable materials, but the detailing should specify surface-finishes and joint-spacing that does not cause difficulty for wheelchair or walker use. Expansion-joints in paving materials should be minimized, and the clear-width should be 1/2" or less when joints are necessary. For the convenience of guests with restricted mobility and for the safety of pedestrians, transitions between finish materials should be flush.

Gratings should not be located on walkways because the slots trap narrow front wheels of wheelchairs, tips of canes or crutches, and women's high heels. If it is necessary to place gratings or drains in the path of travel, the openings should be less than 1/2" wide (in at least one direction) and the pattern of the grating should be aligned such that narrow openings are perpendicular to the direction of travel.

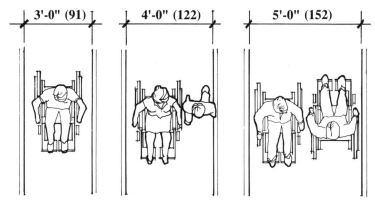

Figure 2.16 A 3'-0"-wide walk meets the minimum requirements for an accessible route. A 4'-0" walk allows ambulatory guests to pass or walk beside guests in wheelchairs. A 5'-0" walk allows simultaneous passage for two guests in wheelchairs, although a width of 6'-0" is recommended.

Raised-edging, or curbs between walks and planting materials, prevent wheelchairs from slipping off the paved surface, but should be at least 4" high to avoid tripping pedestrians. These curbs also help protect guests with restricted vision from potential obstacles such as trees or light posts. Changes in color or paving materials can also define the edges of walks and alert guests to the presence of steps, stairs, or intersecting driveways.

Vertical level-changes should be accommodated by sloped walks, ramps, or mechanical devices such as lifts or elevators. If the slope of a walk is 1:20 or less, special provisions are not necessary. If the slope exceeds 1:20, the walk is considered a ramp. Ramps should have handrails on both sides and meet requirements outlined in ANSI 4.8. Exterior ramps should be covered by canopies or overhangs to prevent the buildup of ice or snow in colder climates. Walks should also be sloped for drain-age; however, cross-slopes greater than 1:50 cause wheelchairs to pull to one side.

Steps or stairs may be incorporated into walks if an alternate accessible route is provided. Stairs should meet requirements in ANSI 4.9. Exterior steps should generally have lower risers (5 3/4" to 6") and wider treads, with an 1/8" per foot slope for drainage. For guests with impaired vision, steps in the line-of-travel should be identified by detectable warning surfaces. (See page 43.)

Lighting is important at walks for both safety and security (minimum 1 footcandle recommended). Lighting, particularly from fixtures below eye level, should be controlled and aimed to reduce glare. Low-level lighting provides better definition to ground surfaces, and therefore is

Raised edging and furniture strip for benches   (2-8)

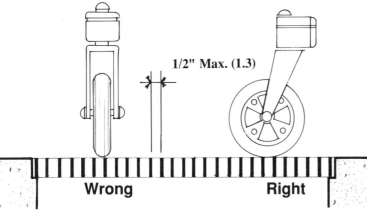

Wrong   **Right**

1/2" Max. (1.3)

Figure 2.17 The front caster-wheels of a wheelchair are solid-rubber, hard-plastic, or pneumatic with a diameter of 5" to 10" and a width of 3/4" to 1 1/4". The wheels are important for maneuvering but vulnerable to wide joints, gratings, and even small vertical-obstructions.

helpful for mobility. Steps or stairs in walks can be high-lighted by low lighting on the surface of the treads, aimed from each side of the steps. This reduces glare, mini-mizes shadows, and visually defines the planes of the treads and risers.

Protected zones that are 6'-8" high and extend the full width of the walk, should be provided for the safety of guests with restricted vision. This zone should be clear of tree branches, wires, signs, and other overhanging elements. Areas with less than 6'-8" of headroom should be protected by guardrails or barriers. (See Figures 2.18 and 3.26.) Site elements, such as light posts, newspaper machines, or benches, can be located in walks if the ob-stacle does not reduce the width to less than 3'-0", and the leading-edge of the obstacle does not extend higher than

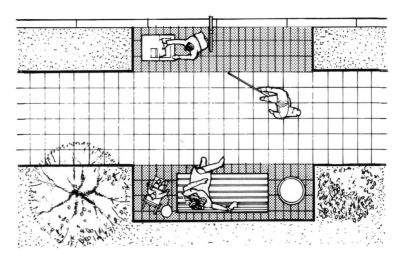

Figure 2.19 Furniture-strips that adjoin walks are recom-mended for site elements such as benches, drinking foun-tains, and trash receptacles. The edge of the strip should be defined by a change in both texture and color.

2'-3" above the ground. This height allows detection with the long-cane technique. Whenever possible, lights and signs should be located in landscape-strips.

Furniture-strips (paved areas adjacent to walks) are rec-ommended to accommodate benches, drinking fountains, phones, trash receptacles, and other site elements. Furni-ture-strips provide access to these elements and maintain a clear path of travel along the walk. Because many guests with restricted vision travel without canes, the edges of furniture-strips should be identified by both a change in materials or texture and a contrasting color.

Figure 2.18 For the safety of guests with restricted vision, a protected zone that is 6'-8" high should be provided. This zone should be clear of low branches, wires, signs, and other overhanging elements.

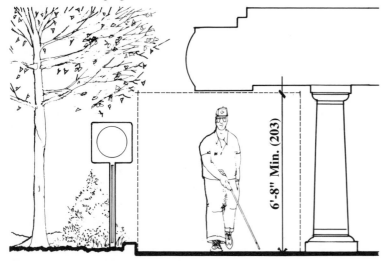

6'-8" Min. (203)

DETECTABLE WARNINGS: Flush-transitions are a potential danger to guests who are blind and use curbs to detect the presence of streets or driveways. Detectable warning-surfaces should be provided to help these guests identify flush transitions (e.g., curb-ramps and driveways). A detectable warning surface is a series of strips or grooves, in a pattern at least 3'-0" wide, that can be detected by the canes of guests who are blind. For exterior use, ANSI requires patterns to be individually-applied strips or surface-applied mats. Warning surfaces should extend the full width of each flush-transition. Caution should be exercised in selecting and installing warning surfaces. If the grooves are too deep or the strips improperly installed, warning surfaces can be hazardous.

Where steps are in the path of travel, warning-surfaces should be provided at the top landing. Changes in the color and pattern of paving materials can also help highlight crosswalks, ramped areas, flush-transitions, and interfaces with vehicular traffic.

NOTE: *Recommendations for the number of accessible elements for site access are provided in Chapter 9, pages 136 and 137.*

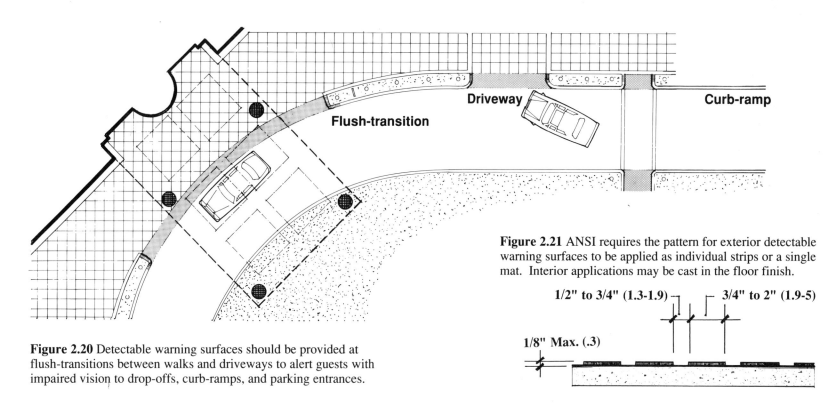

Driveway

Flush-transition

Curb-ramp

Figure 2.21 ANSI requires the pattern for exterior detectable warning surfaces to be applied as individual strips or a single mat. Interior applications may be cast in the floor finish.

1/2" to 3/4" (1.3-1.9) — — 3/4" to 2" (1.9-5)

1/8" Max. (.3)

Figure 2.20 Detectable warning surfaces should be provided at flush-transitions between walks and driveways to alert guests with impaired vision to drop-offs, curb-ramps, and parking entrances.

Property Entrance *(page 26)*

■ An accessible route should be provided from the street, sidewalk, and passenger loading zone to the hotel or motel entrance. *(ANSI 4.3)*

■ If public transportation service is available, an accessible route should be provided from the stop to the hotel or motel entrance. *(ANSI 4.3)*

☐ The entrance to the site and routes to major entrances and parking should be clearly indicated with directional signs.

Passenger Loading Zones *(pages 26 to 28)*

■ Access aisles, at least 4'-0" wide by 20'-0" long, with a slope less than 1:20, should be provided adjacent to vehicular drop-off spaces in loading zones. *(ANSI 4.6)*

☐ For vans or buses with side platform-lifts, an 8'-6" access aisle is recommended for the registration lobby and other major entrances.

☐ Wide flush-transitions are recommended, rather than curb-ramps, at the passenger loading zone for the registration lobby and other major entrances.

■ A canopy, porte-cochere, or overhang is recommended at passenger loading-zones at major entrances to protect guests from inclement weather. Minimum canopy height should be 9'-0". *(ANSI 4.6)* A height of 9'-6" is recommended.

☐ Lighting is recommended at all passenger loading zones for safety and security at night. Higher lighting levels are recommended at major entrances . Large canopies should include skylights to increase natural light during the day.

Parking *(pages 29 and 30)*

■ The number of accessible parking spaces should meet applicable code requirements. Spaces should be located as close as possible to the entrance they serve. *(ANSI 4.6)*

■ Accessible parking spaces should be connected by an accessible route to building entrances. *(ANSI 4.3.2)*

■ Accessible parking spaces should have a minimum width of 8'-0" and an adjoining access aisle 5'-0" wide. The slope of the aisle should not exceed 1:20. *(ANSI 4.6)*

☐ One or more 16'-6"-wide parking spaces are recommended to accommodate side platform-lift vans.

☐ If on-grade accessible parking is not available, the entrance and first floor of parking structures should provide a 9'-0" vertical-clearance for raised-top vans.

☐ Where valet parking is provided, accessible parking should be available for guests to self-park modified vans.

■ All accessible parking spaces should be designated with post-mounted signs. *(ANSI 4.6)*

Curb-ramps and Drives *(page 31)*

■ Curb-ramps should be provided for access to walks from driveways or parking lots. Curb-ramps should be located to preclude obstruction by parked cars. *(ANSI 4.7)*

▨ Curb-ramps should have a minimum width of 3'-0" and a maximum slope of 1:12. Counterslopes and flared-sides should comply with ANSI 4.7.

☐ When site conditions permit, curb-ramps should be recessed into landscape-strips.

☐ Curbs should have a vertical-height of 4" to 6". Crosswalks should connect opposing curb-ramps at driveways.

☐ Lighting is recommended at curb-ramps, crosswalks, and access aisles for safety at night.

Walks *(pages 32 to 34)*

▨ Accessible walks should connect accessible elements by the short and convenient routes. *(ANSI 4.6)*

▨ Walks should have a minimum width of 3'-0" (6'-0" recommended) and a maximum slope of 1:20. Walks should be sloped for drainage, with cross-slopes should be limited to 1:50. *(ANSI 4.3)*

▨ The walk surfaces should be stable, firm, and slip resistant. Transitions or level-changes should be flush whenever possible and no greater than 1/2" in height. *(ANSI 4.5)*

▨ Gratings should not be located in walkways, whenever possible. When this is necessary, gratings should comply with ANSI 4.5.4.

▨ Stairs or steps in walks should comply with ANSI 4.9. Ramps should comply with ANSI 4.8.

▨ Walks should meet headroom and clearance requirements in ANSI 4.4. A furniture-strip is recommended for benches, drinking fountains, trash receptacles, and other site elements located along walks.

☐ Lighting should be provided at walks (minimum 1 footcandle recommended) for safety and security. Low-level lighting is recommended to aid mobility, but should be controlled and aimed to reduce glare.

☐ Contrasting colors and changes in the texture of paving materials are recommended to define edges of walks and highlight interfaces with vehicular traffic.

Detectable Warnings *(page 35)*

▨ Detectable warning surfaces should be provided at flush-transitions between walking surfaces and driveways or streets, and at the top of stairs in walks that are parallel to the path of travel. *(ANSI 4.7 and ANSI 4.27)*

*   *   *   *

Public spaces are important to the visual image of the property.   (3-1)

Chapter 3
Entry, Lobby, and Public Circulation Spaces

Lobbies and public spaces in hotels and motels are used by members of the local community as well as guests making their aesthetic qualities very important to the image of each property. The atrium, first proposed in a 1946 hotel design by Frank Lloyd Wright, has become a popular design element in today's luxury properties. In these often large and complex spaces, it is important that accessible features are designed and incorporated in a manner that does not compromise their aethetic quality.

Because the main entry, lobby, corridors, and public circulation areas are part of an accessible route, specific design details are addressed extensively in the ANSI standard. While much of the relevant material is summarized in this chapter, designers and developers should carefully review applicable local codes to ensure compliance.

In addition to these public spaces, administrative areas such as executive sales and catering offices should also be accessible to visitors.

An entrance is an opportunity to welcome guests. (3-2)

ENTRANCES and VESTIBULES: The design of entrances and vestibules often depends on the local climate and size of a hotel or motel. All guest entrances should have exterior lighting (5 footcandles recommended) and an overhang, for protection, that extends at least 5'-0" in front of the door. To control temperatures and air movement, vestibules are recommended at properties with moderate or severe climates. Natural and artificial lighting in vestibules should provide a balanced transition between the lighting level in the lobby and under the canopy or overhang.

Entrances to the registration lobby may include a combination of manual swinging doors, automatic swinging or sliding doors, or revolving doors. Regardless of the arrangement, at least one door should meet the minimum ANSI requirements for width, operating force, and maneuvering clearances.

ANSI requires that doors provide a minimum clear-open-

ing of 2'-8", calculated by subtracting from the door width, obstructions, such as the thickness of the door in the 90-degree position, the strike-side stop, and offsets for pivot-hinges. (See Figure 3.28.) Because larger doors are more difficult to operate, manual doors should not be wider than necessary.

Because of fire-egress requirements, the width of most entrance doors is 3'-0" or more. However, entry doors are often taller than standard units and equipped with brass hardware and tempered-glass lites. These doors may be heavy and difficult to operate. ANSI specifies that the "pull" or force required to operate exterior doors should not exceed 8 lb. Operating force is a function of the weight of the door and tension applied by closers.

Automatic doors are an effective solution to this problem. These doors are helpful for guests with restricted mobility or limited strength and are also convenient for guests and staff carrying luggage. Automatic doors are available in a number of swinging and sliding configurations that compliment most vestibule designs.

Figure 3.10 Manual vestibule doors in series should include manuevering room between doors. The 4'-0" clearance allows the inside door to swing closed while guests position themselves to open the second door. Additional clearance also provides a better weather vestibule and waiting space.

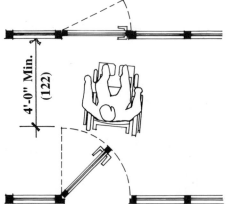

Automatic doors operated by scanner type electronic activating devices eliminate the need for operating mats and awkward guard-rails. Automatic, biparting or revolving doors eliminate problems with swinging doors. For detailed information on automatic doors requirements, see ANSI/BHMA 156.10-1985.

Accessible revolving doors are available in large sizes to accommodate wheelchairs and other assistive devices. Some units are motorized and the speed-of-rotation can be reduced for guests with restricted mobility. Variable speed-controls, or any operating switches, should be mounted in obvious and accessible locations. ANSI requires that revolving doors meet the same requirements as manual swinging doors, unless a second, accessible door is provided.

Manual swinging doors should include maneuvering space to allow guests with restricted mobility to operate the door to both enter and exit. Swinging doors with a front-approach require a 1'-6" clear area (2'-0" recommended) on the strike/pull-side of the door. This clear

Automatic doors are a convenience for all guests. (3-3)

area allows guests to position wheelchairs or other assistive devices clear of the path of the door as it is opened. The clear area should extend 5'-0" in front of the door. If doors have closers and latches, a 1'-0" clear-area is also required on the strike/push-side. Requirements for maneuvering space are described in Figure 3.29. Where doors must be operated in series, additional clearances may be necessary. Clearances for doors in series and 90-degree configurations are illustrated in Figures 3.10 and 3.11.

Thresholds for entry doors should not exceed 1/2" in height and those higher than 1/4" should be tapered or beveled with a slope no greater than 1:2. (See Figure 3.18.) Because of the low thresholds, water penetration can be a problem during wind-driven rain, particularly if doors are not covered by overhangs. If walk-off mats are provided, they should be flush with the top of the threshold or the adjoining floor surfaces. To help prevent falls, floor surfaces in the lobby area should be slip resistant. A minimum coefficient of friction of 0.6 is recommended.

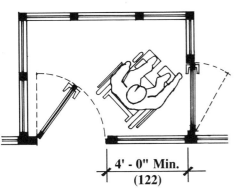
Figure 3.11 Where vestibule doors are provided in a 90-degree configuration, maneuvering clearances should be increased to allow the inner door to close while the outer door is opened.

4' - 0" Min.
(122)

41

The guest's first impression is often formed at the front desk.　　(3-4)

FRONT DESK: The front desk is a symbolic center of a hotel or motel where guests register, pick up messages, seek assistance and information, and pay their bills. From the registration desk, the hotel staff monitors arrivals and departures, oversees seating areas, directs luggage handling, and often supervise hotel operations.

Front desks are usually multilevel counters with worktops at stand-up heights between 2'-7" and 3'-6". The staff area is typically screened with a high counter, which also serves as a writing surface for guests. These counters are often too high to be used by short guests or guests in wheelchairs and present a visual barrier between the guests and staff. Because of the height, the counter cannot serve as a shelf to aid guests to open their purse or briefcase.

Properties can accommodate these guests at a concierge desk or by providing clipboards to serve as writing surfaces. A recommended alternative is a "cut-out" in the high counter. To provide a writing surface, the top of the low counter should project at a height of 2'-10" with a 1'-7"-deep and 2'-3"-high kneespace below. This is the maximum height for guests in wheelchairs and suitable for most staff activities. The cut-out and kneespace should be at least 2'-6" wide, although a width of 3'-0" is recommended.

Task lighting for the high and low counter tops helps guests to read printed material (minimum of 50 foot-candles recommended).

Figure 3.12 A "cut-out" at a registration desk allows for easier communication between staff and short guests or guests in wheelchairs.

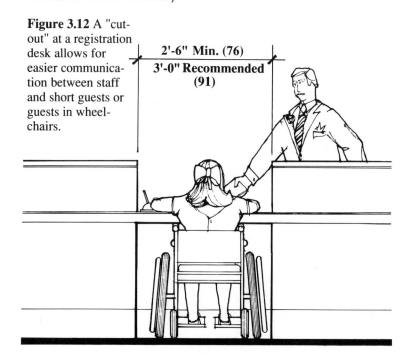

2'-6" Min. (76)
3'-0" Recommended (91)

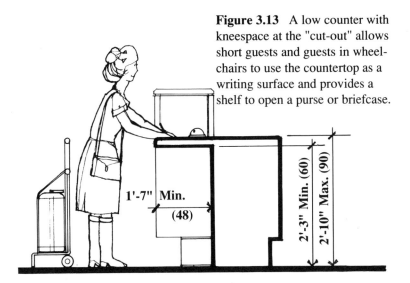

Figure 3.13 A low counter with kneespace at the "cut-out" allows short guests and guests in wheelchairs to use the countertop as a writing surface and provides a shelf to open a purse or briefcase.

1'-7" Min. (48)

2'-3" Min. (60)

2'-10" Max. (90)

SIGNAGE and WARNINGS: Clear and explicit signage throughout each property helps all guests and visitors. Signage should be as consistent as possible in terms of location, mounting heights, colors, typeface, and terminology. For guests with impaired vision, signage pertaining to emergency information, general circulation, and room and space indentification should meet the requirements of ANSI 4.28, which describes the size, proportion, and color of characters, symbols, and backgrounds. These standards are a good guide for all signage.

Signage should be mounted approximately at eye level, and a height of 5'-0" (to centerline) is recommended whenever practical. Signage should be well lit and placed perpendicular to the path of travel, in locations where guests can move closer if necessary to read the lettering.

Graphics, using consistent and commonly recognized symbols, are an excellent technique to communicate information to many guests. Graphics can be read at a greater distance than written signage and are appropriate in many locations.

Raised tactile lettering is required by ANSI for elevator signage. Although raised lettering, particularly smaller characters, are easier to read with tactile senses, the letters or numerals cast shadows under some lighting conditions which may make them more difficult to read visually. At locations such as room identification plaques, where guests can approach and feel the lettering, large, deeply recessed chiselled lettering is an alternative that can be read visually and tactilily.

Figure 3.14 International graphic symbols are easy to understand and also helpful to foreign visitors.

Hazardous areas in public spaces should be identified for the safety of guests with impaired vision. Steps in corridors or lobbies should be preceded by detectable warning surfaces at the top of the run. (See Figure 2.21.) Similar warning surfaces should be provided at the edges of pools or fountains that are not protected by curbs.

Doors from public spaces to hazardous areas, such as loading docks or boiler rooms, should have textured tactile warnings applied to the operating surface of the knob, handle, or pull.

RAMPS and LEVEL-CHANGES: Vertical level-changes in lobbies and other public circulation spaces should be avoided whenever possible. For many older guests and guests using wheelchairs, negotiating even slight inclines can be difficult. Therefore, all basic services should be on one level, if possible. When level-changes are necessary, ramps, elevators, or lifts should be provided for guests with wheelchairs or other assistive devices. Ramps are also more convenient for ambulatory guests carrying luggage.

Ramps are defined as areas with slopes greater than 1:20. Ramps are required to have a minimum clear-width of 3'-0", measured from the inside face of the handrail. This width permits one-way traffic, and is appropriate for short ramps. Where space permits, a 5'-0" width should be provided to allow two guests to travel together or to pass on the ramp. The maximum slope for ramps with horizontal-runs of 30' or less is 1:12. ANSI provides a table indicating the maximum slope for horizontal-runs between 30' and 50'. (See Figure 3.16) Note that the maximum slope is reduced, as the horizontal length of a ramp increases. Continuous ramps should not exceed a total vertical-rise of 2'-6" or a total horizontal-run of 50' without an intermediate landing.

Landings should be at least as wide as the ramp and a minimum of 5'-0" in length. At long ramps (less than 5'-0" in width), 5'-0" wide landings are recommended to allow a guest to wait while another passes. If ramps change direction, the change should occur at a level landing with minimum dimensions of 5'-0" by 5'-0." Ramps should also include level landings at all doors or openings. These landings should be large enough to meet the clearance requirements for door operation for the specific type of door and direction of approach. (See Figure 3.29.)

Figure 3.15 Floor surfaces with a slope greater than 1:20 are defined as ramps. ANSI limits the slope of ramps as a function of the horizontal-run (see chart at right).

Figure 3.16 Table indicating maximum slope and rise for different horizontal-runs.

Slope	Max. Rise	Max. Horizontal-run
1:12 to 1:15	30"	30'
1:16 to 1:19	30"	40'
1:20	30"	50'

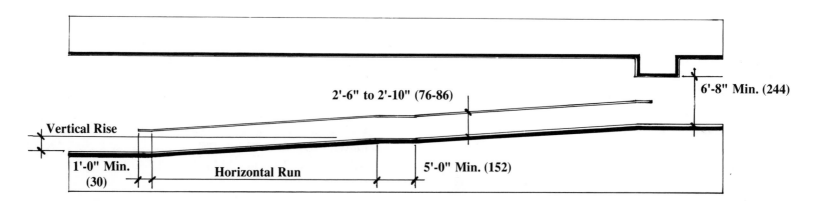

2'-6" to 2'-10" (76-86)

6'-8" Min. (244)

Vertical Rise

1'-0" Min. (30)

Horizontal Run

5'-0" Min. (152)

Ramps and landings adjoining a vertical-drop should be protected by curbs, walls, or railings. If the total vertical-rise of a ramp exceeds 6" or the horizontal-run exceeds 6'-0", handrails should be provided on both sides.

Vertical level-changes cause difficulty for guests in wheelchairs because of the small caster-wheels on their chairs. Even a 1/4" vertical projection can be an obstacle, particularly when wheelchairs are rotating or changing direction. For the convenience of guests with restricted mobility and to reduce accidental trips and falls, flush-transitions are recommended for all floor surfaces.

Vertical level-changes, such as transition-strips between floor finishes, should be less than 1/2" in height. Vertical level-changes less than 1/4" do not require special treatment. Level-changes of 1/4" to 1/2" should be tapered with a slope less than 1:2.

ANSI standards provide good design guidelines for any stair.　(3-5)

STAIRS: Stairs in hotels and motels are used for convenience, as a means of emergency evacuation, and sometimes as an architectural feature. For most guests, including some with restricted mobility, stairs are the best way to get from one floor to another. Stairs, however, are not accessible to guests in wheelchairs and may be difficult for guests with walkers, canes, or limited strength and stamina. ANSI specifically addresses egress stairs and stairs between floor levels not served by elevators.

Maximum slope 1:2

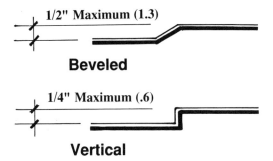

1/2" Maximum (1.3)

Beveled

1/4" Maximum (.6)

Vertical

Figure 3.17 Vertical level-changes of a 1/4" or more should be beveled. Projections higher than 1/2" should be treated as ramps. Whenever possible, transitions between floor finishes should be flush.

Stair risers should be uniform and not more than 7" in height. Treads should have a minimum depth of 11". To avoid falls caused by "hooking" the bottom of a tread, nosings should project no more than 1 1/2" and the underside should be sloped, beveled, or rounded. Open risers are not permitted. Nonslip edges or safety treads are recommended for smooth finishes such as marble, granite, terazzo, or steel-troweled concrete. Handrails should be provided on both sides of all stairs.

Color contrast and lighting can make stairs safer for all guests and particularly for those with restricted vision. Contrasting colors can be applied to treads and risers or used to highlight tread-edges. Where steps occur in the line-of-travel in a corridor or route, a detectable warning surface should be provided at the top of the stair-run to warn guests using canes. (See Figure 2.21.) Stairs should always be well illuminated with diffused light to minimize shadows and glare. A single light source directly overhead can cause glare when ascending stairs and cast shadows in the path of guests who are descending.

High and low handrails can help children. (3-6)

HANDRAILS: Handrails should be provided on both sides of all ramps and stairs to provide either left- or right-side body support and balance. Handrails should be continuous whenever possible, particularly where ramps or stairs change slope or direction. Handrails should not be interrupted by newell-posts or other supporting construction. Where handrails begin and terminate, they should extend past the ramp-segment or stair-run, parallel to the floor surface to allow guests to clear the last step before releasing the rail. (See Figure 3.19.) Handrails should terminate by returning to the wall or supporting post to prevent exposed ends from causing injury or catching loose articles of clothing.

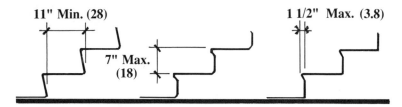

Figure 3.18 Stair risers and treads should meet requirements for height and width. Nosings should be sloped, beveled, or rounded.

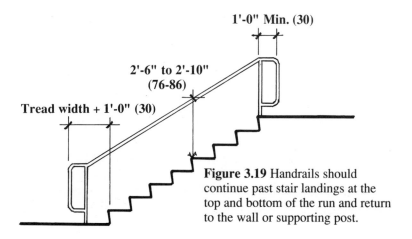

Figure 3.19 Handrails should continue past stair landings at the top and bottom of the run and return to the wall or supporting post.

The gripping-surface of handrails should be equivalent to a 1 1/4" to 1 1/2"-diameter railing. Many codes only permit round railings. Wall-mounted handrails should be separated from the adjoining wall by 1 1/2". To prevent injuries, the wall surface should be free from sharp or abrasive elements. The top of handrails should be mounted between 2'-6" and 2'-10" above the ramp or stair nosing. When appropriate, a lower rail for children can be provided at a height between 2'-0" and 2'-4". For safety at wide stairs, intermediate handrails are recommended.

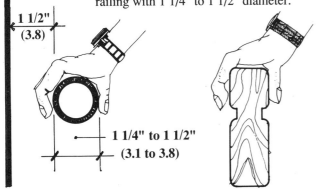

Figure 3.20 Handrails should be configured to provide a gripping-surface similar to a round railing with 1 1/4" to 1 1/2" diameter.

1 1/2"
(3.8)

1 1/4" to 1 1/2"
(3.1 to 3.8)

ELEVATORS: All passenger elevators should include accessible features. For guests with assistive devices, ANSI specifies minimum interior dimensions for cabs and a clear-width of 3'-0" for door openings. Doors should remain open for a minimum of 3 seconds and the operating system should include a time-delayed reopening device activated by low-light sensors. If carpeting is provided in elevator cabs, it should be low-pile and securely fastened. To avoid damage from wheelchair footrests, wall protection is recommended in cab interiors to a height of 9" above the floor. To aid balance, handrails should be provided on the rear and side walls.

Controls in elevator cabs should be located on the front or side wall, depending on the door location. Control panel buttons should be arranged in ascending order with no button higher than 4'-0" above the floor for front wheelchair approach and 4'-6" for side approach. For guests with impaired vision, buttons should be identified with raised tactile numerals or alphabet characters. Buttons should light when pressed and extinguish when the car reaches the desired floor.

The elevator cab floor-location should be visually indicated either above the controls or over the elevator door. For guests using wheelchairs or other assistive devices, who are sometimes unable to turn around in crowded elevators, a mirrored surface on the rear wall of the cab is helpful to read the floor numbers. For guests with impaired vision, audible signals should sound as each floor is passed. Emergency communication equipment should be mounted in accessible locations with instructions for use in tactile lettering.

Floors served by elevators should include call buttons, mounted at a maximum height of 3'-6", that provide a visual indication when calls are registered. Hall lanterns should indicate the arrival of cars and the direction of travel, visually and audibly (one bell for up, two bells for down). For guests arriving by elevator, each floor should be identified on the jambs of the hoistway-door with 2"-high raised numbers at a height of 5'-0".

ANSI provides detailed requirements for elevators.   (3-7)

PUBLIC TELEPHONES: Accessible public telephones should be available in lobbies and other public spaces. For wheelchair access, phones are usually mounted on corridor walls. For a parallel approach, a clear area 2'-6" wide by 4'-0" long should be provided in front of each accessible phone. Telephones should be mounted with the highest operable part, including the coin slot, no more than 4'-6" above the floor. Phones at this height allow both ambulatory and seated guests to dial. At locations with multiple phones, alternative mounting heights can be provided with units more convenient for standing guests (approximately 1'-0" higher). Receiver-handset cords should be at least 2'-5" long and push-button phones are recommended for all locations.

To facilitate conversation and increase privacy, phones should be located away from corridor traffic and other sources of noise. If privacy baffles are provided, the baffles should not project more than 10" or they may

restrict wheelchair access. If the baffles project into corridors more than 4", they should extend below 2'-3" for detection by guests who are blind.

For guests with impaired hearing, telephones should be compatible with hearing aids. Where multiple phones are provided at a single location, at least one phone should be equipped with adjustable volume control and identified with the graphic symbol. These phones are also helpful for guests with speech impairments. For guests who are deaf, a TDD (Telecommunication Device for the Deaf) should be available at the registration desk and so indicated by signage displayed near the public phones.

Telecommunication Device for the Deaf (TDD) (3-8)

A shelf or small counter helps guests using the directory or a portable TDD. Lighting should be provided above the shelf to help guests read the small print (75 footcandles recommended). If directories are permanently attached, the cord should be at least 2'-0" long so guests in wheelchairs can hold the directories in their laps.

House phones should meet the same requirements as public telephones. If house phones are located on desks or counters, kneespace should be provided for wheelchair access. House phones can also be equipped with amplifier hand sets.

Figure 3.21 Wall-mounted telephones should be accessible to guests in wheelchairs. Directories should be conveniently located and a shelf light should be provided to assist guests in reading them. Cords used to attach directories should be at least 2'-0" long so guests in wheelchairs can hold the book close enough to read.

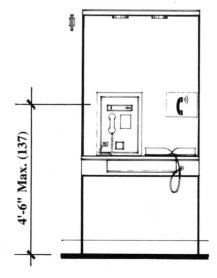

4'-6" Max. (137)

DRINKING FOUNTAINS: Accessible drinking fountains should have spouts no higher than 3'-0" above the floor. The arc of the flow from the spout should be at least 4" above the basin to allow a paper cup to be filled. Controls should be easy to operate and located at the front of the unit. ANSI allows drinking fountains to project for front wheelchair approach or to be recessed for parallel approach. However, parallel approach is more difficult for many guests in wheelchairs because the upper body must be rotated 90-degrees to drink from the spout.

Projecting drinking fountains should include kneespace at least 2'-3" high, 2'-6" wide, and 1'-5" deep. To maneuver into the kneespace, a clear floor area 2'-6" wide by 4'-0" deep is necessary in front of the unit. Projecting drinking fountains that are not recessed into alcoves can be obstacles to guests who are blind. Units can project into accessible routes only if the apron is exactly 2'-3" above the floor. A lower unit does not meet kneespace require-

ments and a higher unit may not be detected by the side-to-side movement of a cane. It is therefore preferable to recess all drinking fountains.

High/low drinking fountains are recommended at all locations to serve both tall and short guests as well as guests using wheelchairs. The maximum height (3'-0") for a single spout is too high for some wheelchair users, yet a lower height is difficult for tall guests or older guests who have difficulty bending over. These projecting units should be recessed in alcoves with the accessible low basin located to provide maneuvering clearances for guests using assistive devices. (See Figure 3.23.)

A cup dispenser in the drinking fountain alcove is convenient for guests who have difficulty drinking from the spout or who need a cup to take medication. Where cup dispensers are provided, trash receptacles are also recommended.

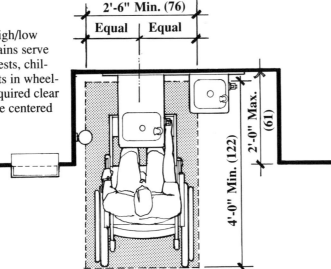

Figure 3.22 High/low drinking fountains serve ambulatory guests, children, and guests in wheelchairs. The required clear space should be centered on the basin.

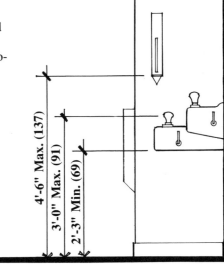

Figure 3.23 Recessed high/low basins are recommended at all locations to serve a range of needs and provide a clear route of travel.

Lobby seating should include a variety of furniture for all guests. (3-9)

LOBBIES and CORRIDORS: Lobbies, corridors, and other public circulation areas in hotels and motels should meet ANSI standards for accessible routes. This requires a minimum width of 3'-0", except at cased-openings or "passage points" (See Figure 3.25.), and greater clearances where an accessible route turns 180-degrees. Doors on accessible routes should provide a minimum clear opening of 2'-8". Clear maneuvering space should be provided for door operation that is appropriate for the specific door type and the anticipated direction of approach. (See Figure 3.29.) Vision panels in corridor doors should be low enough to allow guests in wheelchairs and children to see and be seen (3'-0" or lower recommended). Vertical level-changes should be avoided whenever possible, and ramps or other alternatives should be provided where steps are necessary.

Furniture groupings in lobby seating areas should include space for guests in wheelchairs near tables and lamps. Comfortable chairs or sofas with armrests, firm cushions, and high backs should be available near lamps to provide additional light for reading. For close illumination, the bottom of lamp shades should be at or slightly above eye level which, for most adults, is approximately 2'-6" above the seat. The height should be adjusted for some compression of the seat cushion and the angle-of-recline at the seat and back. Table or floor lamps should be located approximately 1'-8" horizontally from the center of the chair and adjacent to the reader's shoulder to minimize glare.

Figure 3.24 Seating areas should include comfortable chairs located near lamps for reading. Chairs should provide armrests to aid guests to sit and rise.

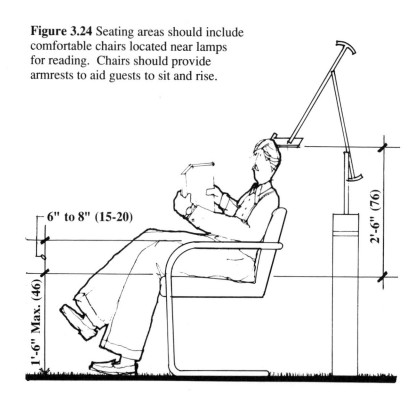

6" to 8" (15-20)

1'-6" Max. (46)

2'-6" (76)

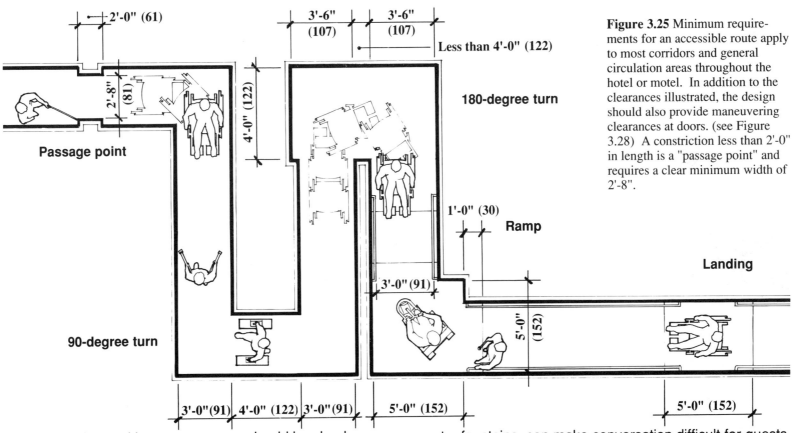

Figure 3.25 Minimum requirements for an accessible route apply to most corridors and general circulation areas throughout the hotel or motel. In addition to the clearances illustrated, the design should also provide maneuvering clearances at doors. (see Figure 3.28) A constriction less than 2'-0" in length is a "passage point" and requires a clear minimum width of 2'-8".

Atrium lobbies and large open areas should be clearly and simply organized to assist orientation and minimize confusion. To help orient guests, changes in floor finishes and color can be used to differenciate between circulation paths and seating or activity areas. For guests who are blind and travel with canes, the unique sound that results from contact with different floor surfaces is important for navigation, especially in undefined open spaces.

Acoustics can be a problem, particularly in large vertical spaces with hard finishes on floors, walls, and ceilings. The "white-noise" from activities or features, such as loud water fountains, can make conversation difficult for guests with impaired hearing and can make travel more difficult for guests with restricted vision who rely on sounds for guidance and orientation. Sound-absorbing finishes and furnishings can help minimize this problem.

Glare in atriums can cause difficulty and discomfort, particularly during certain periods of the day, unless proper sun control is provided. The level of artificial lighting in interior corridors and spaces that adjoin bright, naturally-lit lobbies should be increased to provide a more uniform transition as guests enter or exit the skylit room.

Lobby furniture should allow for unobstructed circulation.   (3-10)

Plants with projecting branches or in hanging baskets with trailing leaves can cause problems for guests with restricted vision. For safety and convenience, plants with foliage that projects beyond the pot or planter should be located away from circulation routes and protected by furniture groupings or defined edges, such as curbs, that can be detected with a cane.

Minimum headroom along accessible routes is 6'-8". Areas with lower headroom should be protected by walls or railings. For the safety of guests with restricted vision, fixtures mounted below 6'-8" such as ashtrays, lighting-sconces, fire extinguishers and trash receptacles, should project no more than 4" into the corridor unless the exposed perimeter of the fixture extends lower than 2'-3" above the floor. (See Figures 3.26 and 2.18.) To avoid abrupt changes in intensity and to minimize shadows,

corridor lighting should provide even levels of illumination (minimum 10 footcandles recommended). Nonreflective wall surfaces and indirect lighting help minimize glare from higher lighting-levels.

Carpeting in corridors should be of low-pile, high density fiber, preferably glued directly to the subfloor without un-layment or installed with high-density padding to allow wheelchairs to roll freely. "Busy" carpet patterns can confuse guests with restricted vision. Changes in the pattern or color of floor finishes should be used to clarify routes-of-travel.

Emergency alarm systems in all public spaces should display both visual signals and sound-audible warnings. ANSI standards include detailed specifications for the sound levels and frequency of audible signals and the flashing frequency of visual signals. Emergency exit instructions should comply with ANSI 4.28.

Figure 3.26 Wall-mounted equipment should not project into corridors more than 4". Similarly, branches should not extend more than 4" beyond the edge of the pot or planter.

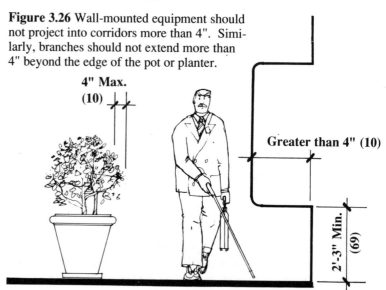

Retail stores should also be accessible. (3-11)

RETAIL: Because of the range of retail activities associated with hotels, it is difficult to establish detailed design requirements. In general, the entrance to shops should meet the requirements for door width and maneuvering space. Level-changes should be avoided when possible and ramped when provided. Display aisles should have a minimum width of 3'-0", and aisle switchbacks and intersections should meet the minimum requirements for accessible routes. (See Figure 3.25.) Sales counters should be as low as possible or include cut-out sections for guests in wheelchairs.

ADMINISTRATIVE OFFICES: Executive offices, sales and catering, and other administrative spaces should be accessible to visitors. Corridors should meet the minimum requirements for accessible routes. Where narrow corri-

dors intersect or change direction, angled corners make maneuvering easier and improve visability. All doors should meet the minimum requirements for width and maneuvering clearances. Private offices should be large enough to provide maneuvering space for visitors with restricted mobility. Accessible toilet rooms should be available to serve these spaces. (See Chapter 8.)

Figure 3.27 To rotate a wheelchair 180 degrees requires a 5'-0"-diameter clear area or a T-shaped clear area to execute a Y-turn. In most cases the 5'-0" circle is more convenient and should be provided when possible. Clear turning spaces are required in restrooms and bathrooms and recommended in any dead-end aisle or passageway.

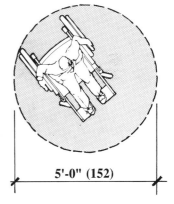

5'-0" (152)

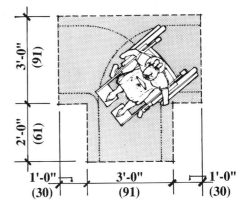

3'-0" (91)

2'-0" (61)

1'-0" (30)   3'-0" (91)   1'-0" (30)

VENDING AREAS and LAUNDRY ROOMS: Vending areas and guest laundry rooms should have 3'-0"-wide doors or a 2'-8" cased-opening and include wheelchair maneuvering space (5'-0"-diameter circle recommended). Vending areas should include a clear-area, 2'-6" by 4'-0", for parallel approach to the machines. For guests with a limited range-of-motion, controls on vending machines should not be higher than 4'-6" or lower than 2'-3". The controls should be easy to operate with limited hand function. In laundries, a clear area should also be available in front of washing machines and dryers. Front-loading laundry machines are easiest for guests in wheelchairs to use but more difficult for older guests. Raised front-loading commercial machine doors are the best alternative.

NOTE: *Recommendations for the number of accessible elements in public spaces are provided in Chapter 9, pages 138-141.*

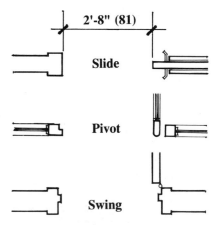

Figure 3.28 The clear opening of any type of swinging door should be measured with the door in the 90-degree position. Stops, door thickness or hinge-offsets should be subtracted from the door width.

NOTES: 1. required if door has closer and latch.
2. 3'-6" required if width is 4'-6"; 3'-0" if width is 5'-0".
3. 4'-0" required if door has closer and latch.
4. 4'-0" required if door has closer.
5. 4'-6" required if door has closer.

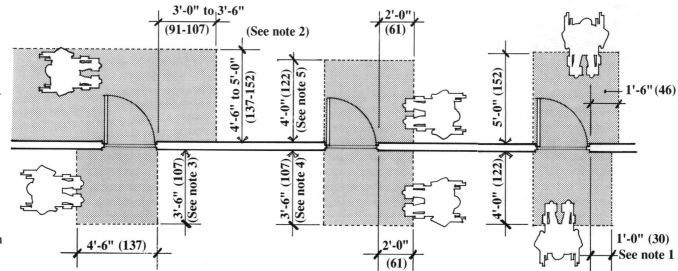

Figure 3.29 Each door requires different maneuvering clearances depending on the direction of the door swing and the direction of approach. Clearances also vary when doors are equipped with closers. Although not an ANSI requirement for all doors, 1'-0" clear area on the latch side always makes operation easier.

Entrances and Vestibules *(pages 40 and 41)*

■ At least one door at each accessible entrance should meet the minimum requirements for width, operating force, and maneuvering clearances. Thresholds at accessible doors should be less than 1/2" in height and beveled or tapered if the height exceeds 1/4". *(ANSI 4.13)*

■ Doors in series should provide the required minimum clearances between doors. *(ANSI 4.13)*

☐ An overhang that extends 5'-0" beyond the door, and exterior lighting (minimum 5' footcandles recommended) is recommended outside all guest entrances.

☐ Weather vestibules are recommended at all guest and staff entrances in properties located in moderate or severe climates.

☐ Accessible automatic doors are recommended at major entrances.

Front Desk *(page 42)*

☐ A cut-out with kneespace is recommended at the front desk. Task lighting should be provided at the writing surface.

Signage and Warnings *(page 43)*

■ Signage pertaining to emergency information, general circulation, and room and space identification should meet ANSI requirements. *(ANSI 4.28)*

■ Stair-runs in corridors should be preceded by a detectable warning surface at the top landing. *(ANSI 4.27)*

■ Doors from public spaces that lead to hazardous areas should have tactile warnings on the operating surface of the door hardware. *(ANSI 4.27.3)*

Ramps and Level-Changes *(pages 44 and 45)*

■ Ramps should have a maximum slope and horizontal-run that meet the requirements illustrated in ANSI 4.8

■ Ramps should have a minimum width of 3'-0" (5'-0" recommended) and handrails on both sides. *(ANSI 4.8)*

■ Where ramps exceed a vertical-rise of 2'-6" or a horizontal-run of 50', intermediate level landings should be provided. The minimum landing width should equal the ramp width (5'-0" recommended), and the length should not be less than 5'-0". *(ANSI 4.8)*

■ Where ramps change direction, level landings should be provided with minimum dimensions of 5'-0" by 5'-0". *(ANSI 4.8)*

■ Where doors are located on ramps, level landings that provide the minimum clearances required for door operation should be provided. *(ANSI 4.8)*

■ Where ramps or landings adjoin a vertical-drop, curbs, walls, or railings should be provided.*(ANSI 4.8)*

■ Vertical level-changes less than 1/4" are permitted. Level-changes between 1/4" and 1/2" should be beveled with a slope less than 1:2. *(ANSI 4.5)*

Stairs *(pages 45 and 46)*

■ Stairs for emergency-egress or stairs connecting floors not served by elevators should meet ANSI requirements. *(ANSI 4.9).*

Checklist: *Entry, Lobby and Public Circulation Spaces*

☑ Risers should be a uniform height not greater than 7". Treads should have a minimum width of 11". Nosings should project no more than 1 1/2", and the underside should be beveled, rounded, or sloped. Open risers are not permitted. *(ANSI 4.9.2).*

☐ The use of color-contrast at nosings or on the surfaces of treads and risers is recommended. Stair lighting should minimize glare and shadows.

Handrails *(pages 46 and 47)*

☑ Handrails should be provided at both sides of all ramps and stairs at a height between 2'-6" and 2'-10". *(ANSI 4.8)*

☑ Handrails should be continuous, wherever possible, uninterrupted by newell-posts or other supporting construction. *(ANSI 4.8)*

☑ Handrails should extend past the top and bottom of a stair-run or ramp-segment parallel to the floor surface. *(ANSI 4.8)*

☑ The gripping-surface of handrails should have a 1 1/4" to 1 1/2" diameter and be mounted 1 1/2" from adja-

Elevators *(page 47)*

☑ Elevator cabs should meet the minimum interior dimensions described in ANSI 4.10. Elevator doors should be 3'-0" wide and equipped with a time-delay activated by a low sensor light. *(ANSI 4.10)*

☑ Elevator control panels, indicator lights, and signals should meet ANSI requirements. *(ANSI 4.10)*

☑ Each floor served by an elevator should include accessible hall buttons and should be identified with 2" raised numbers on the hoistway-door. *(ANSI 4.10)*

Public Telephones *(page 48)*

☑ Accessible telephones should include a clear area 2'-6" wide and 4'-0" long for parallel approach by guests in wheelchairs. *(ANSI 4.29)*

☑ Accessible telephones should be mounted with the highest operable part of the unit at a maximum height of 4'-6". The telephone should be compatible with hearing aids and, if a bank of phones is provided, at least one phone should have adjustable volume control. *(ANSI 4.29)*

☑ Phones that project more than 4" in a corridor should have baffles that extend lower than 2'-3". *(ANSI 4.29)*

☐ House phones should also be accessible and compatible with hearing aids. Push-button phones are recommended at all locations.

Drinking Fountains *(page 49)*

☑ Drinking fountains should have spouts no higher than 3'-0". The arc of the flow from the spout should be 4" above the basin, and the controls should be at the front of the unit. *(ANSI 4.15)*

☑ Drinking fountains designed for front approach should have kneespace below the basin and should be recessed into alcoves. *(ANSI 4.15)*

☑ Drinking fountains designed for parallel approach should have a 2'-6"-wide by 4'-0"-long clear-space in front of the unit. *(ANSI 4.15)*

☐ High/low drinking fountain units recessed in alcoves with cup dispensers and trash receptacles are recommended.

Lobbies and Corridors *(pages 50 - 52)*

■ All corridors and public circulation spaces should meet the requirements for accessible routes. *(ANSI 4.3)*

■ Doors and openings in public circulation spaces should meet the requirements for clear-width and maneuvering space. *(ANSI 4.13)*

■ Emergency alarm systems should display visual and audible warnings. *(ANSI 4.26)*

☐ Open spaces, such as atriums or large lobbies, should be clearly and simply organized with changes in color and floor finishes to define circulation paths.

☐ Sound-absorbing materials should be used in large open lobbies to improve acoustics.

☐ Furniture groupings should include space for guests in wheelchairs and comfortable chairs or sofas with reading lights.

■ The minimum headroom in corridors is 6'-8" and wall-mounted fixtures below this height should not project more than 4" into the path-of-travel. *(ANSI 4.4)*

☐ Corridor lighting should provide even levels of illumination, and glare should be minimized by indirect and controlled lighting and nonreflective surfaces.

☐ Carpeting in corridors and other public circulation spaces should be low-pile, high-density fiber glued directly to the slab or installed with high-density padding.

☐ Carpet patterns and colors should be used to clarify the route-of-travel and highlight obstacles to mobility.

Retail *(page 53)*

■ Doors to retail spaces should meet the ANSI requirements for size and maneuvering space. *(ANSI 4.13)*

■ Aisles in shops should meet the requirements for an accessible route. *(ANSI 4.3)*

Administrative Offices *(page 53)*

■ Corridors and doors in administrative spaces should meet the minimum requirements for an accessible route. *(ANSI 4.3)*

■ Accessible toilet facilities should be convenient to administrative spaces. *(ANSI 4.1)*

Vending Areas and Laundry Rooms *(page 54)*

■ Entrances to vending areas and lavatories should provide at least a 2'-8" clear-opening. A 2'-6" by 4'-0" clear area should be available in front of each machine. Machine controls should be no higher than 4'-6" above the floor and preferably no lower than 2'-3".

☐ A 5'-0" clear turning space should be available within these areas. Raised front-loading laundry machines are recommended.

* * * *

Bedrooms can serve guests with a range of capabilities. (4-1)

Chapter 4
Accessible Guestrooms

Building codes typically require that new hotels and motels provide a minimum percentage of guestrooms that are accessible to physically handicapped guests. Ideally, these guestrooms should allow guests to perform activities with as much comfort and independence as they have in their own homes. Although accessible guestrooms meet the requirements for guests with wheelchairs, the intent is to also provide for the special needs of guests with different types of functional impairments. To meet this objective, accessible guestrooms should be as flexible as possible. For individual guests, staff may need to make minor adjustments to the guestrooms, such as installing portable equipment or removing items of furniture.

Small details often distinguish accessible guestrooms from deluxe guestrooms. With minor modifications, these standard rooms could be classified as "universal" guestrooms suitable for any guest. For a comparison of accessible and standard guestrooms, see Chapter 9.

GUESTROOM PLANS: Accessible guestrooms have design features and floor plans that provide the maneuvering clearances for guests with limited mobility. The following sample plans illustrate guestrooms and bathrooms with the required:

- Widths and clearances at the entry, connecting, closet, and bathroom doors

- Maneuvering space in front of the closet, in the sleeping area, and within the bathroom

- Clearances to use and transfer to fixtures in the bathroom

- Clearances to open dresser drawers, to maneuver into kneespace at the desk, and to access the bed, bedside table, windows, blinds, and thermostat

Clearances may depend on the design of specific furnishings. The width of the access aisle at the bed is determined by the design of the bedside table. Access to dressers is determined by the width of the drawer. The maneuvering space to turn into the desk is determined by the width of the kneespace. (See Figure 5.15.)

The impact of these clearances on the design of most guestrooms with a structural bay-spacing of 13' or greater is minimal. However, in more narrow bay-spacings, the additional area required in the bathroom often affects the layout and function of the sleeping area and the required depth of the bay.

Figures 4.10, 4.11, and 4.12 Bay-spacings of 14', 15', and 16' can easily accommodate guests with restricted mobility. For more detailed bathroom arrangements, see the sample bathroom plans on page 77.

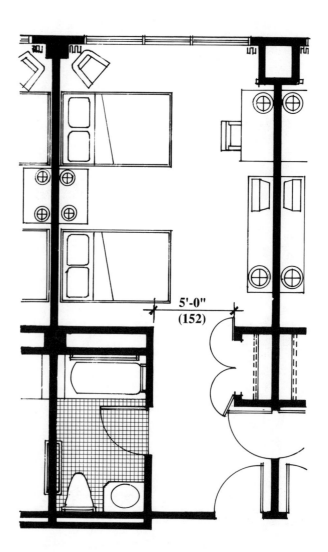

5'-0" (152)

14' Bay-spacing

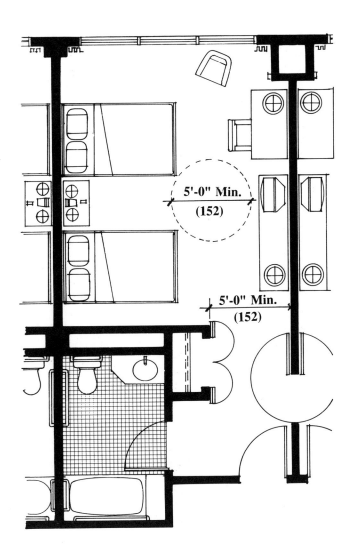

5'-0" Min.
(152)

5'-0" Min.
(152)

15' Bay-spacing

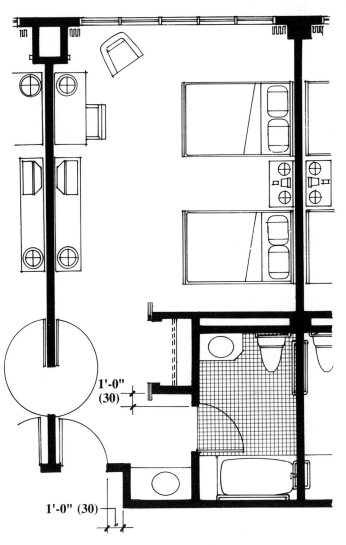

1'-0"
(30)

1'-0" (30)

16' Bay-spacing

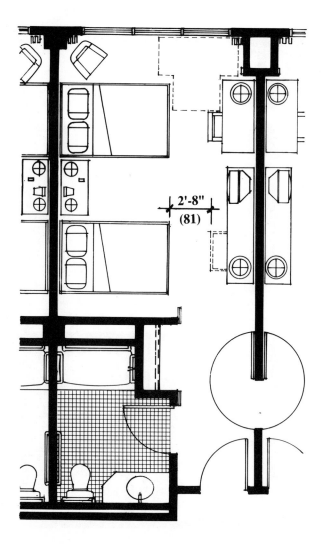

13' Bay-spacing

2'-8"
(81)

Figure 4.13 A 13'-0" bay-spacing provides room for wheelchair clearances, including a turning space in front of the closet and at the foot of the beds, an access aisle between the beds, a T-turnaround at the window aisle for access to temperature controls and blinds and drapes, door clearances, and a bathroom that meets ANSI standards.

Figure 4.14 A 12'-0" bay-spacing may require that one bed be removed from a standard depth room or that the bay depth be increased to accommodate the larger bathroom. The aisle width at the foot of the bed should allow access to the dresser drawers. The bath door can swing into the room if overrun space is available.

Figure 4.15 In an 11'-0" bay-spacing, the critical area is between the foot of the bed (2'-8" passage point) and access to the dresser. The narrow bay-spacing results in a narrower aisle width, therefore the dresser is moved closer to the bathroom to ensure access to the drawers. The furniture arrangement should provide a 5'-0" deep clear space for a front approach to the guestroom door.

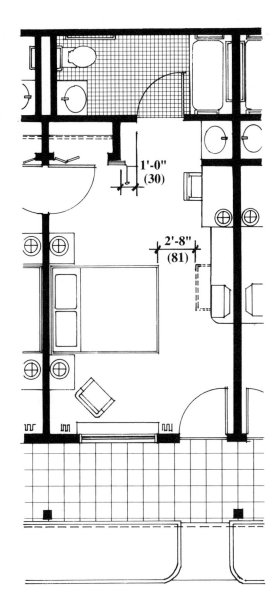

12' Bay-spacing

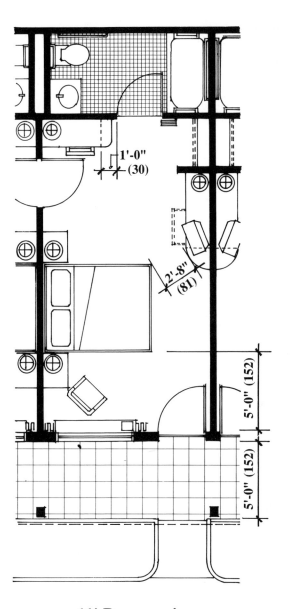

11' Bay-spacing

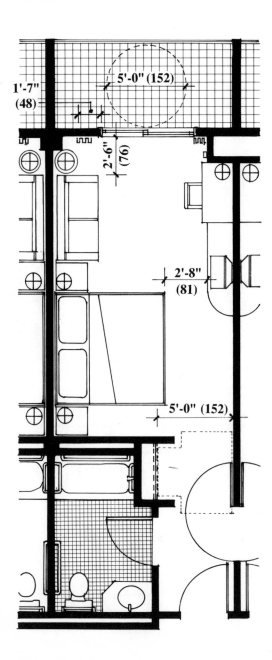

5'-0" (152)

1'-7" (48)

2'-6" (76)

2'-8" (81)

5'-0" (152)

12' Bay-spacing

Figure 4.16 This alternative 12'-0" bay-spacing design requires the dresser to be offset from the foot of the bed. The bathroom wall is stepped back to provide clearances for the bathroom door and connecting door. The heating/cooling unit projects into the room to allow access to the thermostat. If balconies are provided, a minimum depth of 5'-0" is recommended to allow guests with wheelchairs to turn around.

Figure 4.17 Accessible suites should meet the same requirements for accessible guestrooms and guest baths. Because suites are usually more generous in terms of space, providing accessibility is less difficult. If a small kitchenette is included, a kneespace 2'-3" high should be provided below the sink. A countertop height of 2'-10" (2" lower than standard) is suitable for both ambulatory guests and guests in wheelchairs. A pull-out lapboard at a height of 2'-6" provides a workspace for guests in wheelchairs. The kitchenette should include a 5'-0" turning space.

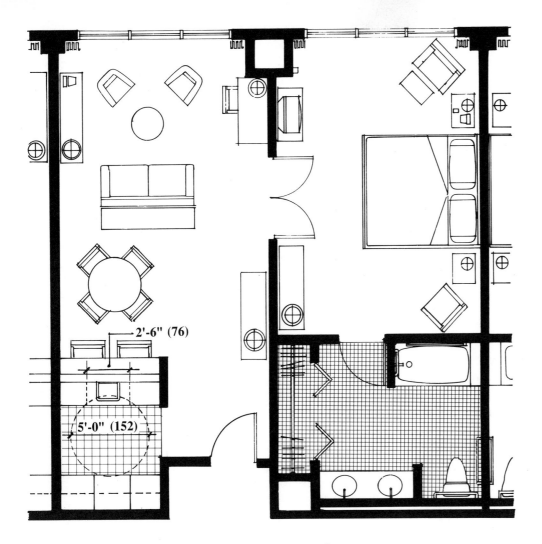

2'-6" (76)

5'-0" (152)

Suite with 14' Bay-spacing

Entry doors with
lever handles and
double security
viewers   (4-2)

Maneuvering space should be provided to operate the entry door. For front approach, a 1'-6" clear space (2'-0" recommended) is required on the pull-side of the door, inside the guestroom. This space allows guests with wheelchairs or other assistive devices, to position themselves clear of the door's path as they pull the door open. A 1'-0" clear space on the corridor/push side of the door is also required if the door has a closer. (See Figure 4.18 and 3.29.) The clear space on the corridor side is recommended at any door to permit guests to angle wheelchairs

GUESTROOM ENTRANCES: Entry doors to accessible guestrooms should be 3'-0" wide to provide a 2'-8" clear-opening, after subtracting the thickness of the door in the 90-degree position and the strike-side doorstop. Lever-type handles should be provided on both sides because the handles are easy to grasp, and are convenient for wheelchair users, older guests, and guests carrying luggage. If doors are equipped with spring-hinges or closers, tension should be adjusted for a maximum force of 5 lb. for interior doors and 8 lb. for exterior doors. If permitted by codes, closers can be omitted.

The height of the threshold or transition-strip should not exceed 1/2" above the adjacent finished floor surfaces, and its profile should be beveled or tapered if the height is 1/4" or more. At exterior entrances, the sidewalk should slope away from the threshold and a roof or overhang should be provided to protect guests and luggage.

Figure 4.18 The 1'-6" clear space (2'-0" recommended) allows guests with wheelchairs and other assistive devices to position themselves clear of the path of the door as it opens. A similar area on the corridor side allows guests to angle wheelchairs to more closely approach the lockset . Ambulatory guests can use this space to center themselves on the lock, to make operation easier.

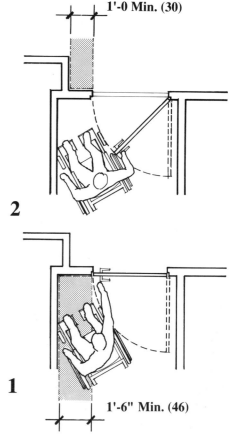

1'-0 Min. (30)

2

1

1'-6" Min. (46)

to more closely approach the lockset. The clear space also allows ambulatory guests to center themselves on the mechanism, which makes the lock easier to see and operate. This additional space also helps reduce damage to doors and the adjoining wall from wheelchair footrests. Connecting doors between accessible guestrooms should be 3'-0" wide with maneuvering clearances and lever handles similar to the entry door.

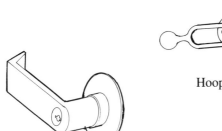

Lever handle

Hoop-type safety lock

Hardware for entry doors should be simple to operate and mounted at convenient heights. Standard locksets or card-entry systems are both appropriate. The time-delay on card-entry systems should be adjusted to allow at least 10 seconds for guests to enter. For guests with a restricted range-of-motion, dead bolts or safety chains should be mounted no higher than 4'-6", and the mechanism should be easy to operate with limited hand function. Operation of the security lock could be critical to guest's safety during an emergency. Hoop-type safety locks, for example, are simple to operate and an effective means of maintaining security. Wide-angle security viewers, or peep holes, should be provided at heights of 3'-6" for guests in wheelchairs, and 4'-9" for ambulatory guests.

Lighting outside the entrances should aid guests in locating the room, operating the lock, and identifing visitors. To help avoid confusion and disorientation, room-identification signage should be prominently displayed and easy to read. For guests with impaired vision, light-colored tactile numerals on a contrasting field, mounted 5'-0" above the floor are recommended. The emergency evacuation instructions on the inside of the door should graphically indicate the room location and exit route. Written instructions should be presented in large, clear lettering (14-point type recommended).

Exterior doors should be protected by a canopy or overhang. (4-3)

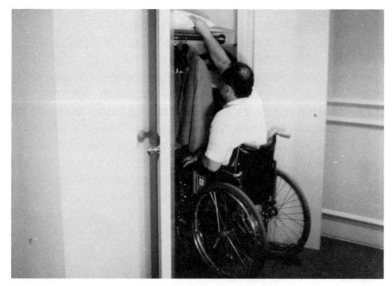

The doors should provide convenient access to closets.   (4-4)

CLOSETS: Access to closets can be difficult for guests with restricted mobility or poor balance. Closet doors can be awkward to operate, particularly in confined spaces, and restrict access to the hanger rods and shelving. Swinging doors require guests to position themselves clear of the swing as the door is opened. Narrow doors (1'-6" or less) minimize this problem. Sliding doors require less clear space to operate but obstruct more than one-half the closet width. Narrow sliding doors and floor-mounted tracks may also restrict guests with assistive devices from partially entering the closet.

Bifold doors that stack flush against the wall are good alternatives for wide closets because they are narrow, easy to operate, and allow access to almost the total width of the closet. Bifold doors do not require floor tracks, allowing carpet to continue into the closet without obstruc-

tion. If guests find bifold doors inconvenient, they can be stacked flat against the wall in the open position for the period of lodging. All closet doors should have pulls that are easy to grasp and catches that provide positive closure but require minimal resistance to operate.

Maneuvering space should be available in front of the closet. ANSI requires a clear space 2'-6" by 4'-0" in front of accessible storage. This space should be increased to allow guests to open and close both closet doors. In general, guests travel from the bedroom to the closet, place or remove clothing, and return to the bedroom area. Because of the space necessary to operate the doors and rotate a wheelchair, a 5'-0"-diameter maneuvering area is recommended in front of the closet.

Figure 4.19 A "split-closet" with a low shelf and rod that can be used by all guests and a high rod suitable for overcoats and long dresses.

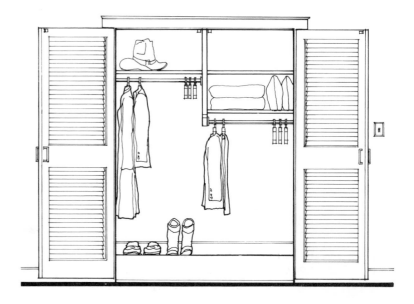

Hanger rods and shelving can be designed to accommodate guests with a range of capabilities. ANSI limits the height of both the pole and shelf to 4'-6", based on the wheelchair user's side-reach. Although these requirements are appropriate, a lowered or adjustable height rod and shelf reduce the flexibility of the closet. A flexible alternative, where space permits, is a "split-closet," with both high and low poles and shelves that offer guests a range of alternatives. (See Figure 4.19.) High hanger rods, while not accessible to some guests, accommodate long dresses, overcoats, and garment bags. This rod can be used by ambulatory guests and guests in wheelchairs with assistance from family or staff. Similarly, a lower shelf and rod are more convenient for all guests with a restricted range-of-motion and easier to see.

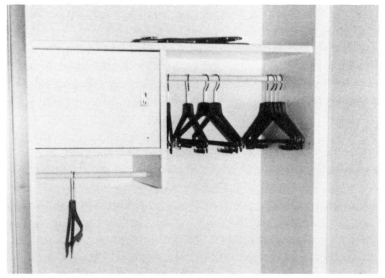

A "split-closet" with a high and low pole and shelf   (4-5)

A raised shoe shelf or platform at a height of 9", no more than 1'-0" deep, provides low storage that is convenient for guests in wheelchairs and guests who have difficulty bending over.

Clothes hangers should be easy to remove and replace. Hangers attached to fixed-rings are more difficult for guests with low vision, limited hand function, and a restricted range-of-motion. Therefore loose, hook-type hangers are recommended.

Lighting should be provided by a fixture in the closet, if codes permit, or in the adjoining passageway. When closets are lit from the passageway, narrow swinging doors or sliding doors may reduce the light level inside the closet.

Figure 4.20 A low shelf serves guests in wheelchairs or older guests. The interior of closets should be well-lit to aid guests with low vision.

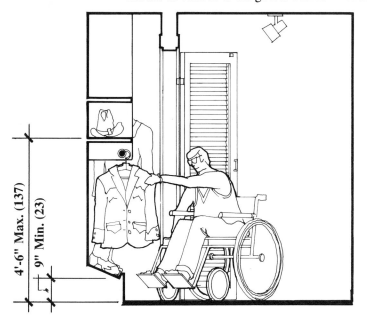

4'-6" Max. (137)

9" Min. (23)

BEDS: The design of beds and their location in the guestroom should allow convenient access by guests with restricted mobility. Bed height should facilitate transfer from a sitting position on the bed to the seat of a wheelchair or to a standing position. For access with assistive devices, a 3'-0" aisle should be available on one side of the bed. To transfer to the bed, guests with wheelchairs use this aisle to back into position, as close as possible to the head, set the brake, drop the arm and footrest, and move from the seat to a sitting position on the mattress.

The height of the bed should be low enough to permit guests' feet to touch the floor but not so low that it is difficult to rise. A height of 18" to 20" from the floor to the top of mattress is recommended. To assist guests in rising, a kickspace, at least 3" high and 3" deep, should be available below the box spring. To facilitate transfer from a wheelchair to the bed, the top of the mattress should match the height of the wheelchair seat, approximately 19" and within the recommended range. For access and comfort, a medium to firm mattress is recommended.

Portable lifts are necessary for some guests who cannot get in to and out of bed independently. An attendant or family member rolls a lift directly over the guest, positioning the floor stand under the bed. Because of the depth of the box spring and mattress, most beds do not provide the 4" to 8" of clearance necessary below the frame. In these instances, beds will have to be temporarily raised with blocking to obtain clearance. The height of the blocking varies with the bed-frame design. With built-in frames, the height of blocking can be reduced if the side panel is removable. Temporary blocking should be securely attached so that it is not inadvertently knocked from under the frame as the lift is maneuvered into position.

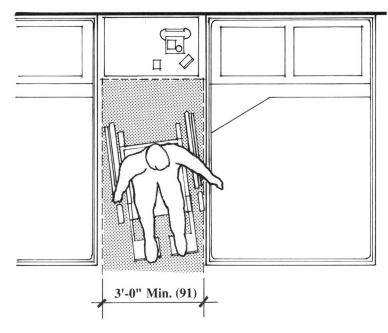

Figure 4.21 Guests with assistive devices need access to the bed for sleeping or relaxing and, in some cases, to change clothing. The aisle beside the bed should be a minimum of 3'-0" wide.

3'-0" Min. (91)

Figure 4.22 In most cases, beds must be blocked up off the floor to allow a portable lift below the frame. Blocking should be attached to the frame so that it is not inadvertently knocked out of position.

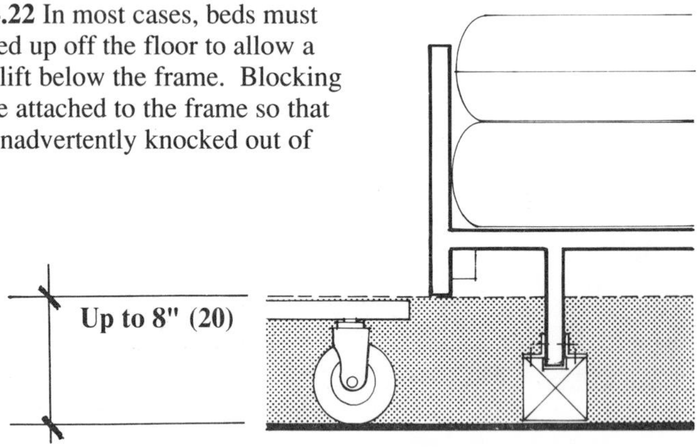

Up to 8" (20)

Figure 4.23 A 4'-0"-wide aisle allows guests to angle a wheelchair or walker to more easily reach the phone. This space also allows a lift to be maneuvered into position below the bed.

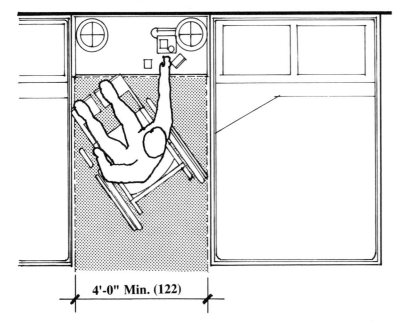

4'-0" Min. (122)

BEDSIDE TABLES: Access to the bedside table is important to reach the telephone or TDD, clock, radio, television controls, and lamps. The design of the table should allow guests convenient access to these items from a sitting position in bed or from the aisle between the beds. For guests seated in bed, the top of the bedside table should be 2" to 3" above the mattress. Access from the aisle is a particular problem for guests in wheelchairs when the aisle width is less than 4'-0". If the aisle is narrower than 4'-0", the wheelchair cannot be angled so that the guest is close enough to reach the telephone or lamp. If a 4'-0"-wide aisle is not available, a 9"-high by 1'-0"-deep toespace can be provided below the table that will allow these guests to approach directly.

Maneuvering space should be available in the sleeping area of the guestroom for guests with restricted mobility. This can be a 5'-0"-diameter circle (recommended) to allow a wheelchair to rotate 180 degrees, or a T-shaped area to execute a Y-turn. (See Figure 3.27.) Maneuvering space can typically be provided by combining the aisle space between the beds and that at the foot of the beds.

TELEVISION and RADIOS: Accessible guestrooms should include remote controls for the television so guests with limited mobility are not required to get into and out of bed to operate the set. Television screens should be as large as practical, located to provide an unobstructed view of the screen, with the center at close to eye level (4'-0") of guests seated in beds or in chairs. To minimize background noise, heating and cooling units should be quiet during operation and located away from the television. For guests with impaired hearing, closed-captioned decoding equipment should be available on request.

Radio/alarm clocks with visual and audible signals and remote outlets to plug-in pillow vibrators or similar devices should also be available to guests on request. The clock face or display digits should be large, well-lit, and easy to read. Control knobs should be easy to grasp and operate.

TELEPHONES: Telephones are important for both convenience and safety. Flashing message lights should be provided on bedside phones to help guests locate the phone in a dark room and to provide a visual indication of incoming calls for guests with impaired hearing. Federal Communications Commission regulations[1] require a minimum of 10 percent of the total guestrooms to be equipped with telephones compatible with hearing aids. These phones can be permanently installed, or compatible handsets can be provided to guests when they register. Amplification handsets with adjustable volume control should also be available on request. Push-button phones are easiest to dial for guests with poor hand function.

For convenience and safety, a telephone should be provided in the bathroom, mounted low on a wall where it can be used to summon help in case of a fall or accident.

[1] Federal Communications Commission, 47 CFD Ch. 1 (10-1-87 Edition), 68.112

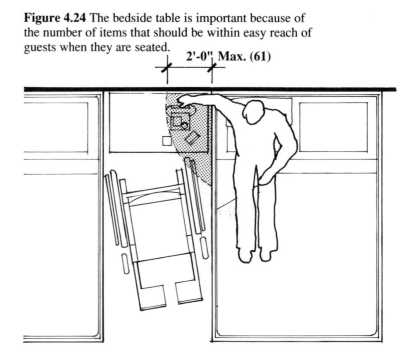

Figure 4.24 The bedside table is important because of the number of items that should be within easy reach of guests when they are seated.

2'-0" Max. (61)

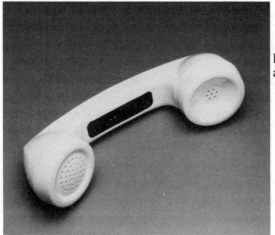

Handset with adjustable amplifier (4-6)

EMERGENCY WARNING SIGNALS: Accessible guestrooms should be equipped with both audible and visual emergency alarm systems. Visual alarms should be designed to flash in conjunction with other building emergency systems and located where the emitted light (or its reflection) is visible from any point in the sleeping portion of the room. Audible alarms should also be installed to provide warnings to guests with impaired vision. (See ANSI 4.26.) To identify guests with restricted mobility in an emergency evacuation, some codes require plaques on the doors or windows of accessible guestrooms. Many guests with functional impairments believe this increases their vulnerability to crime. Therefore, this signage should be available, but displayed at the discretion of the guest.

Figure 4.25 Wheelchair access to the bedside table requires either a 4'-0" aisle or a 9"-high toespace. The top should be 2" to 3" above the mattress. The shade of the reading lamp should be approximately 2'-6" above the mattress.

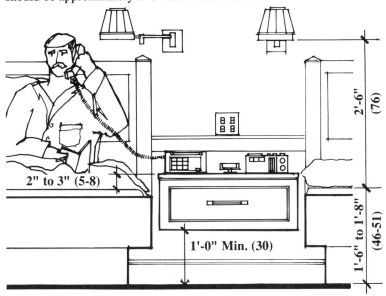

LIGHTING and CONTROLS: Clear access should be provided to all wall switches, lamps, and operating controls. Consolidating switches at appropriate control points, such as the room entry, bathroom entry, and bedside table, makes them easier to locate and access. The use of three-way switches for lighting reduces travel for guests with limited mobility.

Electrical switches should be mounted at a standard height of 4'-0" and controls should be no higher than 4'-6". Electrical wall outlets intended for the use of guests should be mounted in accessible locations at 2'-3" or higher. For example, high outlets can be located near the back of the desktop. Controls, including thermostats, should be easy to operate with limited hand function. Thermostats are often a problem, because many standard units measure room temperature at a height of 5'-0" above the floor. For guests seated in wheelchairs, this is too high to reach and difficult to read because the register is well above eye level. If thermostat sensors can be adjusted, they should be lowered to 4'-6", where they can be read and operated by both ambulatory guests and guests in wheelchairs.

Lamps should have translucent shades to reduce contrast and glare and to provide uniform room lighting. Lamps should be located to provide additional illumination for specific activities such as writing at the desk, reading in a chair, or removing clothing from dresser drawers. Desk lamps should afford guests adjustable lighting levels. For guests with restricted vision or poor hand function, many lamp switches are difficult to locate and operate. In-line cord switches are not recommended, because they require good hand control to operate and often fall behind furniture. Good alternatives are wall switches or touch controls.

Reading lamps should be provided at the bedside table. For close illumination of printed material, the shade of the lamp should be slightly above eye level when seated in bed, approximately 2'-6" above the mattress. Ideally, the intensity and location of the lamp should be individually adjustable. The reading lamp, as well as the telephone, remote controls, alarm clock, and guests' personal effects, should all be within convenient horizontal-reach, approximately 2'-0" from the edge of the bed. To conserve space on the bedside table, wall-mounted lamps are a practical alternative.

FURNITURE and FINISHES: In addition to the bed and bedside table, other furniture and its arrangement are an important part of the guestroom. All furniture should be sturdy and stable, even when weight is applied, because guests often use furnishings for support. In some instances, less furniture may be desirable because more clear floor area is available for maneuvering. On arrival, guests with wheelchairs may request that staff remove desk chairs or other unnecessary pieces of furniture. Furniture should not have sharp corners or projecting legs or crossbars that may trip ambulatory guests or obstruct wheelchair footrests. Chairs should have armrests to aid guests rising from the seat. A portable suitcase stand is an additional furnishing that is helpful to guests with a restricted range-of-motion.

Furniture such as dressers, cabinets, bars, or desks should be easy to access and operate with the use of only one hand. Dresser drawers should be opened with a single center-pull, rather than simultaneous use of two side-pulls. Drawer slides should allow all drawers to operate freely, even with weight in the drawer. The top drawer should be at a convenient height for use by guests with a restricted range-of-motion (2'-3" minimum). To access dressers with wheelchairs or assistive devices, there should be a 2'-8" clear space in front of the face of the drawer when fully opened. The lower edge of mirrors over dressers should be no higher than 3'-6" above the floor.

Cabinets or bars with two narrow doors, rather than a single wide door, are easier to access and operate Desks should provide kneespace at least 2'-6" wide, 2'-3" high, and 1'-7" deep. The desk should have a clear aisle to allow wheelchairs to enter in the kneespace. (See Figure 5.15.) Desk-tops should be no more than 2'-0" deep to allow access to lamps or outlets at the back edge of the top.

Hardware for all furniture should be appropriate for guests with poor hand function. Drawer- or cabinet-pulls should be capable of being hooked rather than grasped. As a minimum, this requires a clear-opening 3/4" deep and 4" long between the pull and the face of the furniture.

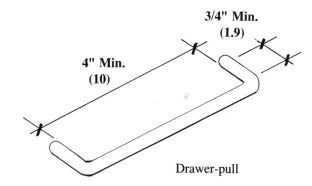

3/4" Min. (1.9)

4" Min. (10)

Drawer-pull

Finishes in accessible guestrooms are very important. Carpet should be low-pile and high-density fiber, glued directly to the slab or installed with a high-density pad, to allow wheelchairs to roll freely. Bathroom floor tile should have a nonskid finish to prevent slips and falls on wet surfaces. Transitions between floor finishes should be as flush as possible. Color contrast between different surfaces and planes of both furniture and finishes aid guests with restricted vision. Protection, such as low corner guards or kick-plates on doors, should be considered in accessible guestrooms to prevent damage to finishes by wheelchair footrests.

Difficult to Operate   **Easy to Operate**

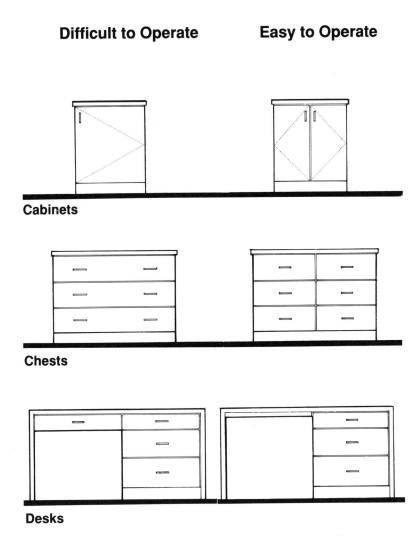

Cabinets

Chests

Desks

Figure 4.26 Two narrow cabinet doors are easier to access than a single wide door. Pulls on low cabinets should be mounted near the top of the strike-side of doors. Narrow dresser drawers with a single center-pull can be operated with one hand. Kneespace at the desk allows guests in wheelchairs to get closer to the writing surface and permits desk chairs with armrests.

WINDOWS and PATIO DOORS: For privacy, and to control natural light and glare, guests should be able to access and operate blinds, sheer curtains, and drapes. Operable windows and patio doors should also be accessible for guests with restricted mobility.

Windows in accessible guestrooms should have low sills and operate with a maximum force of 5 lb. For guests seated 3'-6" from a window, a sill height of 2'-0" allows an unobstructed view 30-degrees below eye level. For guests with restricted mobility, or with limited strength or hand function, double-hung windows are the most difficult to operate. Casement windows with cranks are easier to operate and have the advantage of a single point of control. However, the upper catch on tall casement units may be above the vertical-reach of some guests. Low awning windows, below fixed lites, are easy to access and can also be operated with one hand. Sliding windows with good roller systems are excellent units but require a long, horizontal clear space to operate.

Doors to patios or balconies may be sliding or swinging units. Sliding doors should not be too large or heavy and the threshold at the guide-tracks should be beveled or tapered with a maximum height of 3/4". This threshold height is permitted by ANSI as a special exception. All doors should provide a 2'-8" clear opening and have handles and locks that are easy to grasp and operate. Swinging doors to patios should meet the same requirements for hardware and maneuvering space as the entry door.

Window treatments should be controlled from accessible locations. To operate most drapes, a rod must be moved from the closed position, in the center, to each side of the window, which requires a clear path of travel for the full-width of the window. Drawstrings for blinds, sheer curtains, or drapes should be attached to the floor or side wall in a manner that keeps them visable and accessible. Where furniture or heating and cooling units restrict access, heavy drapes that cannot be operated by drawstrings may require motorized controls.

The bathroom should include clear access to the tub/shower.   (4-7)

GUEST BATHROOMS: Guest bathrooms should provide maneuvering space for guests with restricted mobility, including clearance for door operation, an unobstructed turning space, and required clearances for each bathroom fixture. Because of the vertical characteristics of wheelchairs, these clearances can incorporate kneespace or toespace below vanities or water closets. All requirements for clear maneuvering space can overlap.

Doors to accessible baths were traditionally designed to swing out because there was insufficient maneuvering space in the bath for wheelchair users to execute a 180-degree turn, which required guests to back out of the room. Out-swinging doors also eliminated the possibility, in the event of an accident, that the door would be blocked. Both are more likely occurrences in undersized baths. ANSI does not require bathroom doors to swing out, and in most cases, it is unnecessary. If doors swing into the room, an overrun space, 2'-6" by 4'-0", should be available for guests with wheelchairs to position them-

Figure 4.27 Overrun space, 2'-6" by 4'-0", is also required to allow guests in wheelchairs to clear the door-swing while closing the door in the bathroom.

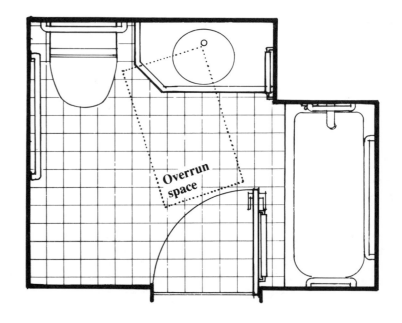

selves clear of the door while closing it. Bathroom doors should have a minimum width of 3'-0" and lever handles.

Supplemental heat, such as radiant heat lamps, should be provided in bathrooms with exterior walls at properties in cold climates. Wall heating units should not be used unless thay are protected to prevent inadvertant contact by guests.

Figures 4.28 and 4.29 These two figures illustrate the same bathroom plan with the required clearances for door operation and turning space and access to each fixture, including the tub/ shower, vanity, and water closet. Clearances for maneuvering space, door operation, and individual fixtures can "overlap." Because of the vertical characteristics of wheelchairs, clearances can include toespace (9" high) below water closets and kneespace (2'-3"high) below vanities.

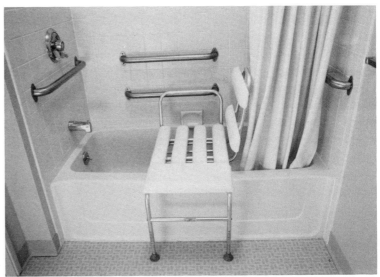

Shower seats should be available on request.   (4-8)

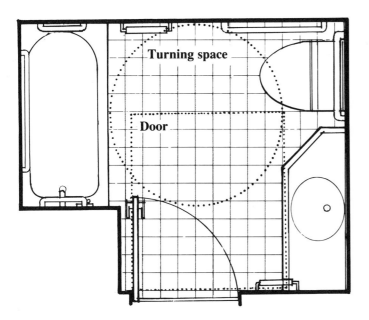

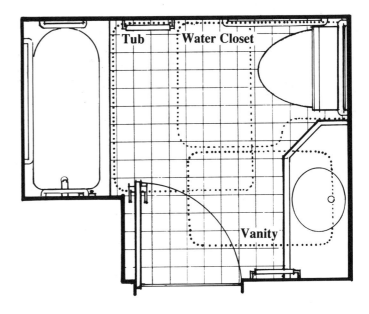

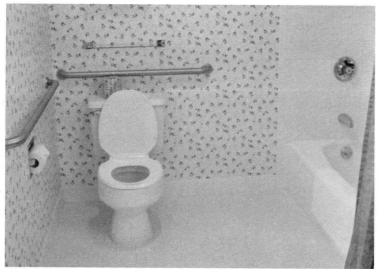

Water closets should have grab bars to aid balance and transfer. (4-9)

WATER CLOSETS: The bathroom arrangement should allow guests with restricted mobility to access the water closet. Guests with wheelchairs can transfer to the seat of the water closet using one of three methods: front, diagonal, or side transfer. Diagonal or side transfer are the most common methods. ANSI illustrates two configurations to provide access to water closets. (See Figures 4.31 and 4.32.) Arrangement A allows diagonal or side transfer and provides greater flexibility to accommodate guests' individual preferences and capabilities but requires more space. Arrangement B only permits diagonal transfer. Clearances also vary for front or parallel approach.

In either arrangement, grab bars and toilet paper dispensers should be installed as illustrated in Figure 4.30. Wall-hung water closets are recommended, particularly in small bathrooms, because they provide additional maneuvering clearance (3" or more). All maneuvering clearances can

include available toespace (minimum height 9") below the water closet or any bathroom fixture.

The height of water closet seats is important, in assisting guests to sit and rise and for wheelchair transfer. ANSI specifies an acceptable range of 17" to 19" above the bathroom floor, higher than the standard 15" to 16" seat height. A height of 19" is convenient for wheelchair transfer, because it closely matches the height of most wheelchair seats. This height is less convenient for ambulatory guests, particularly older guests with impaired balance. The best alternative is a water closet with the seat 17" high . If necessary, staff can raise the height for individual guests, using spacer rings under the toilet seat.

Figure 4.30 Grab bars and toilet paper dispensers should be mounted as illustrated. These grab bars aid balance and wheelchair transfer.

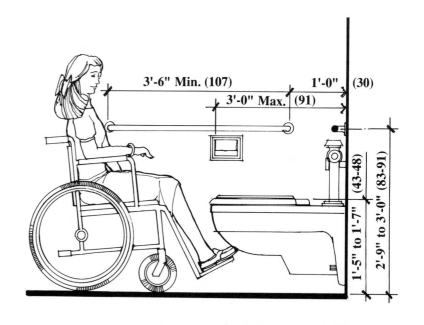

A. Side transfer

Figure 4.31 Minimum clearances for side transfer from a wheelchair to the seat of the water closet with front or parallel approach.

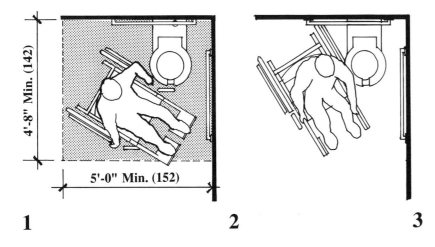

4'-8" Min. (142)

5'-0" Min. (152)

1

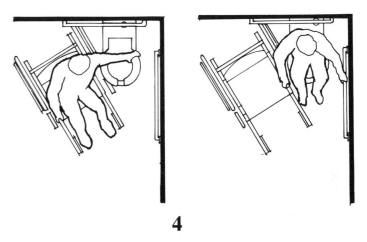

2

3

4

B. Diagonal transfer

Figure 4.32 Minimum clearances for digonal transfer from a wheelchair to the seat of the water closet with front or parallel approach.

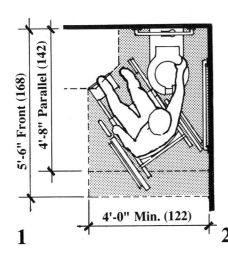

5'-6" Front (168)

4'-8" Parallel (142)

4'-0" Min. (122)

1

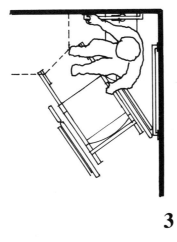

2

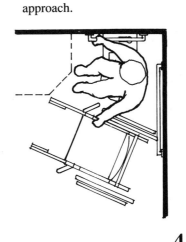

3

4

An accessible vanity with kneespace and tissue dispenser.   (4-10)

VANITIES: The vanity, basin, and mirror in accessible baths should allow guests to wash, shave, apply makeup, and perform other activities associated with grooming. For wheelchair access, vanities should have kneespace below the apron with minimum dimensions of 2'-3" high*, 2'-6" wide, and 1'-5" deep. The kneespace height can be reduced incrementally, following the profile of a wheelchair. (See Figure 8.11.) Exposed hot-water pipes, drains, or sharp or abrasive surfaces that abut the kneespace should be insulated or protected. For guests in wheelchairs, a clear area 2'-6" wide by 4'-0" deep should be provided in front of the vanity.

Vanity tops should be as shallow as possible, not more than 2'-0" deep, to allow guests to reach items at the back

*Kneespace at lavatories should be 2'-5" high. As a partial enclosure, a vanity apron can be 2'-3" high.

edge. Shallow tops also permit guests with low vision to get closer to the mirror and light to shave or apply make-up. A cut-off or mitred corner on the top improves access to adjacent toilets and also permits closer access to the mirror without leaning across the vanity.

For guests with restricted mobility, hand towels and facial tissues should be within convenient reach of guests positioned in front of the basin. Tissue dispensers can be located in the vanity apron or recessed in the adjacent wall. An electrical outlet (GFI) should also be located at the side wall, within easy reach of guests standing or seated in front of the vanity.

Basins should be mounted with the rim at a height of 2'-10". The bowl should be shallow, no deeper than 6 1/2",

Figure 4.33 The vanity should include kneespace below the basin. The height of the kneespace can be reduced incrementally (also see Figure 8.11).

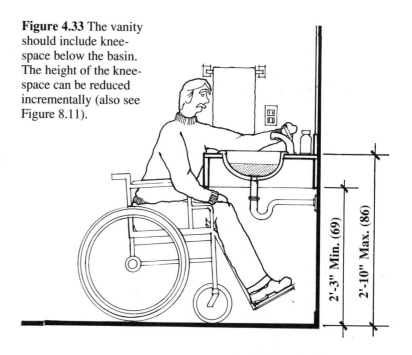

2'-3" Min. (69)   2'-10" Max. (86)

and an oval shape is recommended. Faucets should be easy to operate with limited hand-function. Lever-type faucets or single-lever controls are recommended. For guests with restricted vision, "hot" and "cold" should be clearly identified with graphics, color, and/or tactile symbols. A hand-held spray is recommended to permit guests who have difficulty showering or bathing to use the basin to wash their hair.

Mirrors should be mounted to serve guests in wheelchairs and ambulatory guests. The ANSI minimum for the height of the lower edge of the mirror is 3'-4". Because eye level for guests in wheelchairs is 3'-6" to 4'-3", mirrors should be lower whenever possible. The top of the mirror should extend to a minimum height of 6'-2". Where space permits, full-length mirrors are recommended in the bath or dressing area.

The tub/shower should help guests to safely bathe or shower.   (4-11)

Figure 4.34 The kneespace below the vanity should be at least 2'-6" wide. A mitred corner on vanity tops adjoining toilets allows guests to more closely approach the mirror.

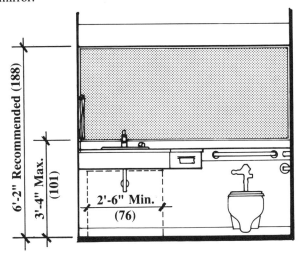

TUBS and SHOWERS: The design of the tub/shower unit and the bathroom plan should permit guests to bathe or shower in a standing or seated position. In most cases, the critical activity is getting into and out of the tub, particularly for bathing because guests must move from a standing position to a sitting position.

Access to safely enter and exit the tub/shower and to adjust the temperature controls before bathing or showering is critically important. To ensure access, clear maneuvering space should be provided for the full length of the tub. For guests with restricted mobility, ANSI requires a clear area 2'-6" wide for parallel approach and a 4'-0"-wide clear area for front approach. Because approach is usually perpendicular to the tub, a 4'-0" clear area is recommended. Glass sliding doors should not be substituted for shower curtains, because they restrict access and the tracks on the tub rim interfere with wheelchair transfer.

ANSI illustrates a lavatory "dotted-in" adjacent to the foot of the tub. (See Figures 4.35 and 4.36.) However, this arrangement is not recommended because it restricts access to the temperature controls and prevents ambulatory guests from entering the shower near the spray head and temperature controls.

Tub/shower units can be conventional 5'-0" tubs or a tub with a built-in 15" seat. Either tub can be used for bathing or showering by ambulatory guests or guests with restricted mobility. The built-in rear seat provides ambulatory guests with an alternative method of getting into and out of the tub for bathing and also serve~ as a convenient shelf for shampoo, toiletries, or towels. Both tubs should be equipped with grab bars on the foot and back walls.

The conventional tub should also include a grab bar on the head wall. (See Figure 4.39.) Either tub should include a hand-held shower spray.

To bathe, ambulatory guests can step over the rim of the tub and lower themselves to a sitting position, using high or low grab bars on the back wall as aids to balance. If a built-in seat is provided at the foot of the tub, guests can sit on the seat and swing their legs into the tub before lowering themselves into the water.

Guests with wheelchairs approach the tub perpendicular to the rim, position their feet in the tub, reach across to the low grab bar on the back wall and lower themselves into the tub. Though the guest is aided by the buoyancy of the water, this activity requires both upper body strength and agility.

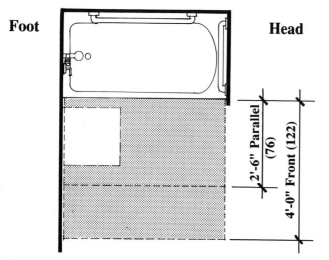

Figure 4.35 A 5'-0" tub/shower can be used for bathing and showering either in the standing position or on a portable seat. A 4'-0"-wide clear area is recommended for front approach.

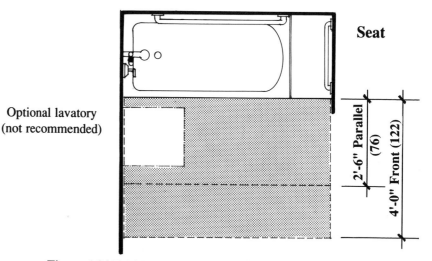

Figure 4.36 Tub/shower with a built-in seat allows guests to seat themselves and swing their legs into the tub before lowering their body into the water. The seat can also serve as a shelf for toiletries or towels.

Figure 4.37 Wheelchair transfer (front approach) to a portable shower seat for showering. The seat is positioned near the center of the tub so guests can reach the controls.

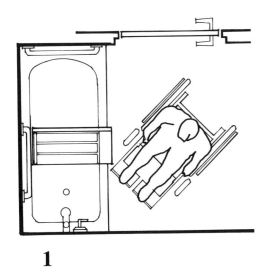

1

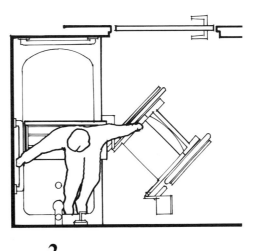

2

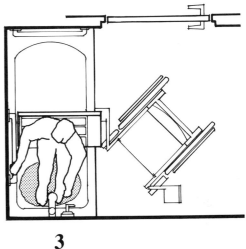

3

Figure 4.38 Wheelchair transfer (front approach) to a tub for bathing. Clear access is required to allow guests to close the drain and draw the water before transferring to the tub.

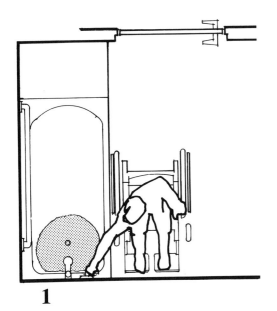

1

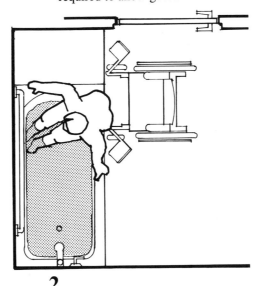

2

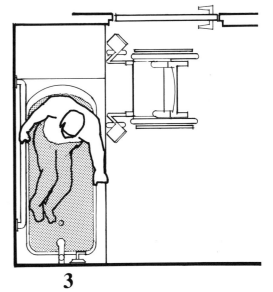

3

To shower, guests with wheelchairs transfer to a portable shower seat positioned over the tub. From the portable seat, the water temperature is adjusted and the spray discharge is switched from the faucet to the hand-held shower head. To reach the temperature controls, the portable seat should be positioned near the middle of the tub. This procedure is more difficult if a lavatory is located adjacent to the tub on the foot wall. (See Figures 4.35 and 4.36.)

Ambulatory guests should be able to enter the tub for showering with the aid of a grab bar to maintain balance. Entry is safest at the foot of the tub, near the temperature-controls, where the wall of the tub is vertical. A high grab bar should also be provided on the back wall as an aid to balance during showering. For safety, the bottom of the tub should have a nonslip surface.

Roll-in shower with a low
curb.   (4-12)

Tubs/showers should include both high and low recessed soap dishes, large enough for shampoo or toiletries and convenient for guests who are showering or bathing. Unless a light fixture is provided over the tub, shower curtains should be translucent to increase the light level with the curtains drawn. Towels should be convenient to guests exiting the tub, on racks or bars mounted 4'-6" above the floor.

Roll-in showers are preferred by many guests with wheelchairs because they allow users to remain in special wheelchairs while showering. Roll-in showers should be 4'-0" by 4'-0" with low curbs and a small portable ramp or flush threshold. Showers are considered safer for older guests, because thay do not require users to move from a standing to a sitting position. These are excellent alternatives for properties that provide showers instead of a tub/shower combination or for larger properties with a mix of room types.

Controls for tubs and showers should include remote drain controls and mixing valves with single-lever handles, which can be operated with one hand. Whenever possible, the controls should be offset toward the edge of the tub for easier access from outside the unit. Mixing-valve temperatures should clearly indicate "hot" and "cold" with graphics, color, and/or tactile symbols. The hand-held shower spray should have a 5'-0" hose and vertical slide to allow operation in a high, fixed position. In preparing rooms for guests with wheelchairs, the staff should ensure that the hand-held shower spray is set in a low position. Extremely hot water is a danger to everyone, but guests with restricted mobility and limited tactile senses are most vulnerable. The maximum hot-water temperature in the bathroom should be limited to 120 degrees F.

BATHROOM LIGHTING: Overall bathroom lighting should be adequate for safety and mobility (minimum 30 footcandles recommended). A higher lighting level should be provided at the vanity and mirror to allow guests to perform fine hand function and see to apply makeup (minimum 70 footcandles recommended). A full-spectrum fluorescent fixture with a baffle and prism lens provides diffused lighting and flattering skin tones. The use of matte-finishes, where practical, reduces the glare from walls and fixtures and color contrast helps guests see fixture edges and grab bars in monochromatic bathrooms, where guests often remove their eyeglasses.

GRAB BARS and BATHROOM ACCESSORIES: Grab bars should be provided at water closets, tubs, and showers. Grab bars should have an outside diameter of 1 1/4" to 1 1/2", mounted 1 1/2" from the finished wall surface. If grab bars are mounted further from the wall, the user's hand can accidentally slip between the wall and the railing. To avoid injuries, wall surfaces behind grab bars should not have sharp or abrasive finishes. Backing plates or similar devices should be installed in walls to provide anchorage to meet the structural requirements in ANSI 4.24.3. Grab bars are available in a variety of colors and finishes, including nonslip patterns for use in wet areas. Towel bars should be mounted in convenient locations that allow access for guests with restricted mobility. Racks located above water closets, for example, are not accessible. Robe hooks mounted at 4'-6" can be used by all guests.

NOTE: *Recommendations for the number of accessible elements in guestrooms are provided in Chapter 9.*

Figure 4.39 Grab bars should be installed at tub/showers as illustrated.

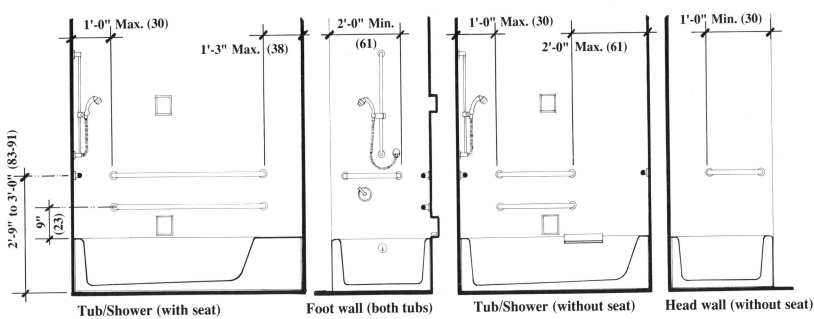

Tub/Shower (with seat)   Foot wall (both tubs)   Tub/Shower (without seat)   Head wall (without seat)

Guestroom Entrances *(pages 66 and 67)*

■ Guestroom doors should have a minimum width of 3'-0" and lever-type handles. Spring-hinges or closers should be adjusted for a maximum force of 5 lb. for interior doors and 8 lb. for exterior doors. *(ANSI 4.13)*

■ The entry should include manuevering space inside and outside the room for door operation. *(ANSI 4.13.)*

■ Thresholds or transition-strips should be no higher than 1/2". The profile should be beveled if the height exceeds 1/4". *(ANSI 4.13)*

■ Safety chains, dead bolts, and other hardware should not require fine hand control to operate and should be mounted no higher than 4'-6". *(ANSI 4.13)*

☐ High and low security viewers should be installed in the guestroom door at heights of 3'-6" and 4'-9".

☐ The entry should be well-lit (minimum 10 footcandles recommended) and room-identification signage should be clearly displayed and easy to read.

Closets *(pages 68 and 69)*

■ Maneuvering space should be provided for closet door operation and to allow guests in wheelchairs to turn around after using the closet (5'-0"- diameter recommended). *(ANSI 4.13)*

■ Hanger rods and shelving should be no higher than 4'-6" above the floor. *(ANSI 4.23)* A "split-closet with both high and low shelving is recommended.

■ Low shelving for shoes should be provided at least 9" above the floor. *(ANSI 4.23.3)*

☐ Clothes hangers should be easy to remove and replace. Hangers attached to fixed-rings are not recommended.

☐ The interior of closets should be well-lit.

Beds *(page 70)*

☐ A 3'-0"-wide aisle should be provided on at least one side of the bed. The recommended height for beds is 18" to 20" measured to the top of the mattress.

☐ Blocking should be available to raise the bed frame to accommodate portable lifts.

Bedside Tables *(page 71)*

☐ If the access aisle to the bedside table is less than 4'-0" wide, the table should provide toespace at least 9" high and 1'-0" deep.

☐ The location of the bed and overall guest room arrangement should provide a 5'-0"-diameter clear space or T-shaped area to rotate a wheelchair.

Televisions and Radios *(page 71)*

☐ Televisions should be equipped with remote controls at the bedside table. The screen should be as large as practical and displayed with the center at approximately eye level (4'-0") for seated guests.

☐ Closed-captioned decoding equipment should be available to guests on request.

☐ Alarm clocks or radio alarms with visual and audible signals should be available on request.

Telephones *(page 72)*

☐ Telephones compatible with hearing aids should be provided or compatible handsets should be available to guests on request (see note page 72).

☐ The bedside telephone should be equipped with a message-flash light. Amplification handsets with adjustable volume control should be available on request.

☐ As a safety measure, a telephone is recommended in the guest bathroom.

Emergency Warning Signals *(page 72)*

▣ Accessible guestrooms should be equipped with audible and visual alarm systems. *(ANSI 4.26)*

☐ Plaques to identify accessible guestrooms should be available to guests who wish to display them on doors or windows.

Lighting and Controls *(page 73)*

▣ Switches should be mounted at a height of 4'-0". Controls should be mounted no higher than 4'-6". *(ANSI 4.25)*

▣ Electrical outlets should be mounted no lower than 1'-3" above the floor. *(ANSI 4.25)* High outlets (2'-3" minimum) are recommended for guests with a limited range-of-motion.

☐ Lamp switches should be easy to locate and operate. Wall switches or touch controls are recommended.

☐ Reading lamps should allow individual guests to adjust the intensity.

Furniture and Finishes *(page 74)*

☐ Furniture should be easy to access and operate. Hardware should be capable of being hooked rather than grasped.

☐ Carpeting should be low-pile and high-density fiber, glued directly to the subfloor or installed with a high-density pad.

☐ Color contrast in finishes and furnishings should be used to help define surfaces and planes.

☐ Bathroom floor tile should have a nonskid finish.

Windows and Patio Doors *(page 75)*

▣ Sliding or swinging doors to balconies should meet ANSI requirements for clear-width, maneuvering space, threshold and hardware. *(ANSI 4.13.5)*

☐ The guestroom arrangement should provide access to operable windows, doors, blinds, drapes, and other window treatments.

☐ Where viewing is important, low window sills (2'-0" or lower) are recommended for seated guests.

Guest Bathrooms *(page 76 and 77)*

▣ Bathrooms should include a clear turning space, either a 5'-0"-diameter circle or a T-shaped clear area. *(ANSI 4.22)*

▣ The bathroom should include maneuvering clearances for door operation. If the door swings into the bathroom, an overrun space should be provided to allow the wheelchair to clear the swing of the door. *(ANSI 4.22)*

Water Closets *(pages 78 and 79)*

■　Water closets should be located to provide clear access for at least one method of wheelchair transfer. *(ANSI 4.16)*

■　The top of the water closet seat should be between 17" and 19" above the floo.r *(ANSI 4.16.3)* A height of 17" is recommended and spacer rings should be available on request.

■　Grab bars and toilet paper dispensers should be installed as described in ANSI 4.16.4 and ANSI 4.16.6.

Vanities *(page 80 and 81)*

■　Vanities should include kneespace below the apron and basin with minimum dimensions of 2'-3" high, 2'-6" wide, and 1'-7" deep. Hot-water pipes or sharp or abrasive surfaces that abut the kneespace should be insulated or protected. (ANSI 4.19)

■　The top of the basin should be no higher than 2'-10". The basin should be no deeper than 6 1/2". *(ANSI 4.19)*

□　Vanity tops with a depth between 1'-10" and 2'-0" are recommended with a mitred corner when the vanity adjoins a water closet.

■　Mirrors should be mounted with the lowest edge of the reflecting surface no higher than 3'-4". *(ANSI 4.19)* Whenever possible, lower heights are recommended.

■　Faucets should be easy to operate with lever handles or single-lever controls. *(ANSI 4.19)* Hand-spray attachments and remote drain controls are recommended.

Tubs and Showers *(pages 81-84)*

■　Tub/showers should provide clearances for front or parallel wheelchair approach. *(ANSI 4.20)* Whenever possible, it is recommended that clearance for front approach be provided.

■　Tub/shower units should include grab bars to assist wheelchair transfer and aid balance. *(ANSI 4.20)*

■　Showers should be equipped with curtains rather than sliding doors. *(ANSI 4.20)* Translucent shower curtains are recommended to increase lighting with the curtains drawn.

■　Seats at tubs should be built in or portable shower seat should be available on request. *(ANSI 4.20)*

□　For properties that provide showers or offer alternatives to tub/shower units, roll-in showers are recommended in accessible bathrooms.

■　Roll-in showers should meet the requirements of ANSI 4.21.

■　All tubs or showers should have an offset single-lever mixing valve, hand-held shower head, and remote-control drain. *(ANSI 4.21.4, 4.21.5)*

Bathroom Lighting *(page 85)*

□　The overall lighting level in the bathroom should be adequate for safety and mobility (30 footcandles minimum recommended).

□　The lighting level at the vanity should allow guests to perform fine hand function, shave, and apply makeup (70 footcandles recommended).

Grab Bars and Bathroom Accessories *(page 85)*

▨ Grab bars should have an outside-diameter of 1 1/4" to 1 1/2" and be mounted 1 1/2" from the face of the wall. Wall anchorage should meet the requirements of ANSI 4.24.

☐ Towel bars, hair dryers, robe hooks, and other accessories should be mounted in convenient and accessible locations no higher than 4'-6" above the floor.

*   *   *   *

Armrests aid in sitting and rising and provide arm support.   (5-1)

Chapter 5
Restaurants and Lounges

Restaurants and lounges in hotels and motels serve guests, members of the community, and corporate and professional groups using meeting facilities. Designs for these spaces are often determined by furniture and furnishings rather than by architectural elements such as walls or doors. Therefore, most building codes are less definitive in terms of precise design requirements for these spaces.

The ANSI standard does not specifically address restaurants and lounges but includes a section on built-in seating and counters and illustrates clearances for chairs and tables. Requirements for accessible routes should also be met, and the design of elements in restaurants and lounges should reflect the capabilities for forward- and side-reach of customers as described in ANSI 4.4.

The design of restaurants and lounges often responds to economic forces to achieve maximum seating capacities as well as to marketing requirements for interesting and exciting interiors. With careful planning and selection of furnishings, finishes, and lighting, these spaces can be accessible, efficient, and attractive.

RESTAURANT and DINING ROOM SEATING: Dispersed seating suitable for guests with restricted mobility should be available in restaurants, coffee shops and dining facilities. As a guide, the Uniform Federal Accessibility Standards (UFAS) require a minimum of 5 percent of restaurant seating to be accessible. Accessible aisles should connect the entrance to these seating locations, public restrooms, and self-service areas such as salad bars, condiment stands, or buffet tables. Comfortable seating for waiting should be available to customers near the entrance.

A variety of accessible seating should be available, suitable for large and small dining groups. Small tables may not be accessible to guests in wheelchairs because of the restricted kneespace. Therefore, a party of one or two may require a table usually set up for four. Restaurants or coffee shops with built-in seating, such as booths or banquettes, should also provide some chairs for guests who have difficulty getting into and out of bench seating.

Figure 5.10 Restaurants or coffee shops with fixed seating should include some movable seating for guests in wheelchairs and guests who have difficulty getting into and out of the bench seating.

These chairs can be removed to seat guests in wheelchairs. Where seating areas are raised on platforms, accessible seating and similar services should be available on the main-floor level or a ramp to ther upper level should be provided.

Aisles serving accessible seating should be at least 3'-0" wide, which typically requires a 6'-0" clearance between parallel tables, or 4'-6" between rotated tables. (See Figure 5.11.) Aisle widths should also provide room for customers to be seated at tables. At least a 2'-6" clear space should be available behind each seating location. This space allows chairs to be withdrawn from the table and staff to assist guests reposition chairs close to the table.

For wheelchair seating, a 3'-0" to 3'-6" aisle is necessary, depending on the width of the kneespace. (See Figure 5.15.) Wheelchairs positioned at tables project approximately 5" further into aisles than most chairs. To allow guests with restricted mobility to turn around, seating arrangements should also include a 5'-0" diameter circle or T-shaped clear area at dead-end aisles. (See Figure 3.27.)

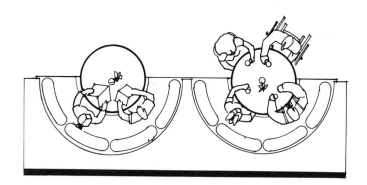

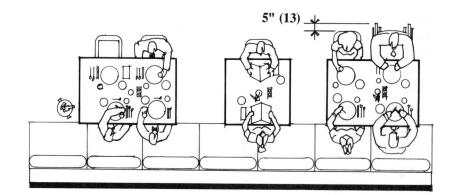

5" (13)

Restaurants and lounges should offer a variety of seating.   (5-2)

DINING TABLES and CHAIRS: Accessible seating locations should allow guests with restricted mobility to dine with ambulatory customers. Tables should provide kneespace for customers in wheelchairs, and dining chairs should be coordinated to provide comfortable seating at the same table height.

Dining room chairs should be stable to maintain balance as guests seat themselves, and comfortable to sit in during dinner. Chairs should be light and easy to reposition. The seat should have a slight slant to the rear to transfer body weight to the back of the chair. However, an exaggerated incline makes it difficult to rise. The seat should be approximately 16" deep and at least 16" wide to allow space for customers to reposition themselves during the meal. Padding or cushions on the chair seat should be firm, and the chair back should also be slightly inclined to the rear. To help guests sit and rise, dining chairs

should have armrests 7" to 8" above the front edge of the seat. (See Figure 5.12.) Supports or cross-bracing should not interfere with kickspace below the seat, so the feet can be positioned to rise. The front edge of the chair seat should be low enough to allow the feet to rest on the floor, but not so low that it is difficult to rise. This is determined by the lower leg length (popliteal height) which varies between 15" and 20" for most adults.

The height of the chair seat should be 10 1/2" to 11 1/2" below the top of the table. Common seat heights vary between 14" and 18". Because the height of wheelchair

Figure 5.11 Aisles serving accessible seating should provide a path at least 3'-0" wide for passage and clear space for guests to seat themselves at tables.

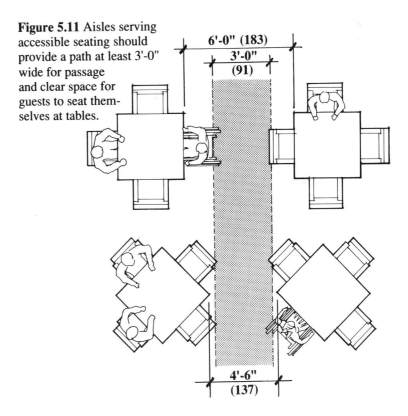

seats is typically 19", a relatively high chair seat is necessary to coordinate with the table height. A chair with an 18" high seat is comfortable for most ambulatory guests and closely approximates the height of a wheelchair seat.

Dining room tables should have a stable surface at a convenient height and kneespace and legroom below the tabletop for customers in wheelchairs. Narrow table configurations allow face-to-face seating, which reduces the distance between diners, making conversation easier and table lighting more effective. For safety, the corners and edges of the top should be rounded.

Full-height wheelchair kneespace is 2'-6", which requires tabletops to be at least 2'-7" above the floor, too high for most seating. Many wheelchairs now provide adjustable or two-tier armrests, which allow customers to sit close to tables in a kneespace only 2'-3" high. To provide this kneespace, the tabletop (without an apron) should be 2'-4 1/2" to 2'-5" above the floor. This is 11" to 11 1/2" above the chair seat, 10 1/2 to 11" above the seat of wheelchairs, and convenient for both. This kneespace also permits the armrests of chairs to pass below the tabletop so seated customers can draw close. This combination of tables and chairs is suitable for the majority of wheelchair users and most ambulatory guests.

A portable raised leaf should be available to modify tables for customers in wheelchairs with high armrests. The leaf should be approximately the size of a place setting, 1'-4" by 2'-0", and secured to the underside of an accessible table with clamps. The raised leaf should project 6" beyond the edge of the table and provide 2'-6" clearance above the floor. (See Figure 5.14.)

Footroom is important for customers with wheelchairs or leg braces. The footrests of wheelchairs are 2 1/2" to 3" above the ground and angled slightly forward, which requires 1'-7" of footroom, measured from the edge of the tabletop. The outside width of footrests is only 1'-6", but

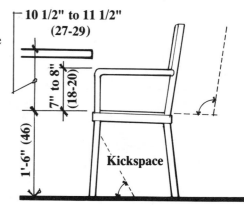

Figure 5.12 Dining room chairs should have a seat 10 1/2" to 11 1/2" below the top of the table and armrests 7" to 8" above the seat.. To coordinate with an accessible table, the seat height should be 18".

Figure 5.13 Accessible tables should provide kneespace at least a 2'-3" high by 2'-6" wide with 1'-7" of footroom. To increase the kneespace height, a raised portable leaf can be provided. (See Figure 5.14.)

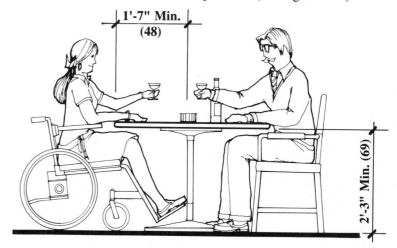

2'-6" of side-to-side clearance is necessary to maneuver into position beneath the table. To provide kneespace, table legs should be at least 2'-6" apart, and the tabletop, for face-to-face seating, should be 3'-6" wide. Pedestal-base tables should have low, tapered bases and a minimum diameter of 3'-6", although 4'-0" is preferred.

Figure 5.14 A portable raised leaf can be provided for accessible tables to accommodate customers in wheelchairs with high armrests.

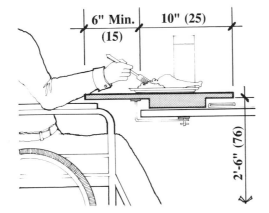

6" Min. (15)   10" (25)

2'-6" (76)

Figure 5.15 The necessary maneuvering room required to access a kneespace depends on its width.

Kneespace Width	Clearance
2'-6" (minimum)	3'-6"
3'-0" or greater	3'-0"

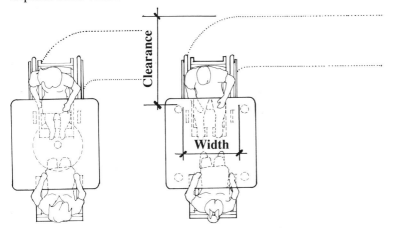

Clearance

Width

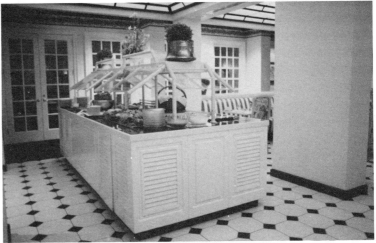

Salad bars should assist customers to serve themselves.   (5-3)

SELF-SERVICE AREAS: Salad bars, buffet lines, condiment stands, and other self-service areas should be accessible. Cafeteria or food-service lines should have a minimum width of 3'-0", but a width of 3'-6" is recommended to permit ambulatory customers to pass customers in wheelchairs.

The tray slide should be 2'-10" above the floor, the maximum height for customers in wheelchairs and convenient for ambulatory guests. The tray slide should be continuous, if possible, from the entrance to the cashier. Tray slides restrict access to the counters and therefore should not be wider than necessary (1'-0" recommended). In this instance, the reach of a customer in a wheelchair is extended if the wheelchair can be angled or positioned perpendicular to the tray slide. This is possible if the lower face of the counter is recessed to provide low kneespace. (See Figure 5.16.)

Figure 5.16 Cafeteria lines should be wide enough to accommodate guests in wheelchairs. Food and beverages should be within a convenient vertical- and horizontal-reach.

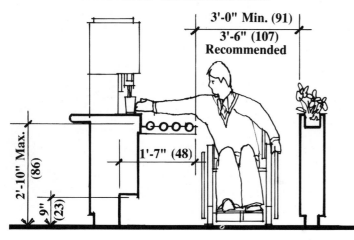

Figure 5.17 A plate slide is recommended at salad bars and a kneespace at the counter. (See Figure 8.11.) A mirrored surface above the bar is a further aid to guests in wheelchairs.

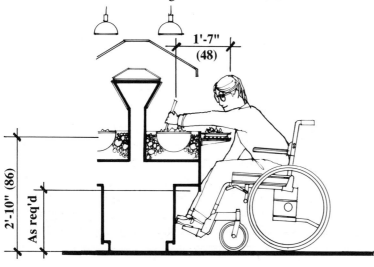

For guests with a limited range-of-motion, food, beverages, utensils, or other items should be displayed near the edge of the counter where they are easier to see and reach. When duplicate items are displayed, a vertical rather than horizontal arrangement allows customers to select items at the most convenient height. Self-service systems, such as beverage or ice-dispensers, should be easy to operate without fine hand function. Instructions and price information should be prominently displayed in large clear lettering.

Salad bars and buffets should provide a 3'-0"-wide clear space for access on all sides and plate slides, or areas to temporarily set plates, at a maximum height of 2'-10". This permits customers to serve themselves with one hand, without simultaneously balancing the plate or bowl. Kneespace 2'-3" high below the counter or table, allows front wheelchair approach, to increase customers' forward reach. Condiments should be located as low and close to the edge of the counter or table as practical. A tilted-mirror above the food display at salad bars also aids customers in wheelchairs and children. (See Figure 5.17.) For some customers with restricted mobility, poor balance, or limited hand function, it is more difficult to carry a plate. Therefore trays should be available at both salad bars and buffets.

TABLEWARE and ACCESSORIES: Tableware and other accessories should be selected for ease of use, particularly for guests with limited strength or poor hand function. Flatware or utensils with large-diameter handles are generally easiest to grasp. Four-pronged forks are easier to use than three-pronged forks. To reduce spills, glassware and cups should have broad, stable bases. Cups or mugs should have handles that are large and easy to grasp. Glasses with a pattern or texture usually provide more surface friction and therefore a firmer grip. Drinking straws should be available on request. Utensils and glassware should be symmetrical for easy use by right- and left-handed customers.

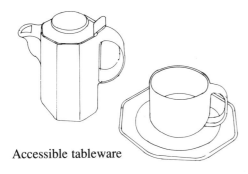

Accessible tableware

Pitchers and carafes should be small, lightweight, and easy to use. Lids for coffee or teapots should be attached and simple to operate, preferably with one hand. Some prepackaged condiments such as crackers, jellies, or cream can be difficult to open with limited hand function. Alternative means of providing these items should be considered. For customers with impaired vision, menus should be easy to read, with a simple layout, large typeface (14-point or larger recommended), and clear contrast between the text and background colors. A matte finish is recommended to reduce glare. Braille menus should also be available.

An accessible bar with a low top and low stools　　　(5-4)

LOUNGES AND BARS: Entrances to lounges and bars should be accessible to guests with restricted mobility. Aisles should provide accessible routes to connect the entrance, seating locations, public restrooms, and the dance floor. Tables and chairs for food service should meet the dining room requirements described in the previous sections.

Continental or lounge seating, common in many bars and lounges, is not suitable for customers with restricted mobility or poor balance. Low chairs or sofas, particularly those with soft cushions, make it difficult to sit or rise, and the size and weight of these chairs make them difficult to reposition. Tabletops lower than the seat height are also more awkward to use. Lounges should include some chairs with firm cushions at a height of at least 17" and adjacent tabletops 7" to 8" higher than the seats.

The height of most bar tops prevents their use by customers in wheelchairs. High bar stools are also difficult for some ambulatory customers with a restricted range-of-motion or poor balance. For these customers, similar services should be available at nearby accessible seating.

Some properties provide low continental bars with the bartender's work area lowered and chairs or low stools for customers. With minor modifications (See Figure 5.18), these bars can be accessible to guests in wheelchairs and also provide seating that is convenient for other guests.

Figure 5.18 A continental bar with low seating is accessible to more customers. The bartender's area can be lowered or the seating area can be on a raised platform accessible by a ramp.

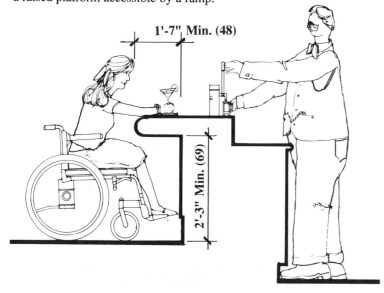

Table lighting helps customers read the menu.   (5-5)

LIGHTING: Lighting levels and patterns are important in establishing the ambiance for a restaurant or lounge and for the safety and comfort of customers, particularly those with restricted vision, impaired balance, or limited agility. Lighting requirements for any room depend on many factors, including the color and reflectance of the surfaces, the contrast between objects and backgrounds, and the direction of the light. The overall lighting level in restaurants or lounges should always be adequate to allow safe movement throughout the facility. Additional lighting should highlight potential hazards, such as steps or ramps.

Variations in lighting intensity and patterns can be used for orientation and aesthetic effect, but the general lighting level should be reasonably consistent, without disconcerting changes in intensity that require rapid readjustment of

Good acoustics help increase privacy between adjacent tables.   (5-6)

the eyes. Natural light from windows or skylights should be controlled to avoid excessive glare.

Task lighting should be provided at tables for activities, such as reading a menu. Table lighting also aids guests with impaired hearing who depend on lip reading. For older customers, who may require more than twice the normal level of illumination, portable supplemental lighting can be provided. Task lighting for reading or eating is most convenient if both the intensity and location can be adjusted by the customer.

FINISHES: Special finishes are not required in lounges or restaurants. However, certain finishes and transition conditions should be carefully detailed and specified. Carpeting should be low-pile, preferably glued directly to the slab or installed with a high-density pad, to allow wheelchairs to roll freely. The edges of area rugs should be tapered or recessed flush with the adjoining finish to avoid obstructing wheelchairs or tripping ambulatory guests. Area rugs should be firmly secured to avoid rippling, that makes travel with assistive devices more difficult. In areas subject to spills and mop-up, recommended floor surfaces should be slip-resistant (minimum coeffcient of friction 0.6 wet/dry). In restaurants and lounges with hard surface finishes for walls, floors, and ceilings, sound-absorbent material should be used in furnishings to reduce background noise and reverberation, which make conversation difficult, particularly for guests with impaired hearing. Kitchen noise should be minimized by locating service away from seating areas. Sound systems for live or recorded music should be adjustable.

NOTE: *Recommendations for the number of accessible elements in restaurants and lounges are provided in Chapter 9, pages 146 and 147.*

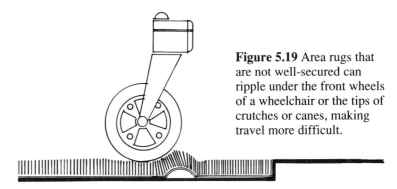

Figure 5.19 Area rugs that are not well-secured can ripple under the front wheels of a wheelchair or the tips of crutches or canes, making travel more difficult.

Restaurant and Dining Room Seating *(page 92)*

■ Provide accessible routes to connect the entrance, accessible seating locations, self-service areas, restrooms, and telephones. (*ANSI 4.3*)

■ Provide accessible tables and seating locations for customers with restricted mobility. (*ANSI 4.1 and AH&MA Interpretive Guide*)

Dining Tables and Chairs *(pages 93 and 95)*

☐ Provide accessible tables suitable for large or small groups, with compatible chairs for ambulatory guests.

☐ Chairs should be stable and lightweight and have firm cushions and armrests. At accessible tables, a seat height of 18" is recommended.

☐ Accessible tables should provide at least a 2'-3"-high kneespace and 1'-7"-deep legroom. The top of the table should be 2'-4 1/2" to 2'-5" above the floor.

☐ A portable raised leaf should be available on request for customers in wheelchairs with high armrests.

Self-Service Areas *(pages 95 and 96)*

☐ Provide accessible self-service areas such as cafeteria lines, salad bars, and condiment stands.

☐ Cafeteria lines should be a minimum of 3'-0" wide, with a tray slide no higher than 2'-10". A low kneespace is recommended at the counter for wheelchair access.

☐ Food, beverages, and utensils should be displayed as low and close to the edge of the counter as practical.

☐ Plate slides or areas to temporarily set plates are recommended at salad bars and buffets. A low recess at the counter should be provided to improve wheelchair access. Trays should be available.

Tableware and Accessories *(page 97)*

☐ Consider ease of use in selecting glassware, china, utensils, and other tableware and accessories.

☐ Menus should be easy to read with a clear contrast between text and background colors, large, simple typeface (14-point or larger), and a matte finish.

Lounges and Bars *(pages 97 and 98)*

■ Provide accessible routes to connect the entrance, accessible seating locations, restrooms, telephones, and the dance floor. *(ANSI 4.3)*

☐ Provide accessible seating locations for customers with restricted mobility.

☐ With continental or lounge seating, also provide some furniture groupings that are more suitable for customers with limited strength, balance, and mobility.

☐ If a low bar is provided, the design should include a bartop height and kneespace appropriate for customers in wheelchairs.

Lighting *(pages 98 and 99)*

☐ Provide adequate lighting levels to ensure safe movement throughout the facility. Use lighting to highlight potential hazards to mobility, such as steps or ramps.

☐ Natural light from windows or skylights should be controlled to reduce glare.

Finishes *(page 99)*

☐ Carpeting in accessible areas should be low-pile. Area rugs should be securely fastened, particularly at the edges, and recessed flush, if possible.

☐ Hard floor surfaces in wet areas should be slip resistant. (.06 coefficient wet/dry)

☐ Sound-absorbent materials in furnishings and finishes are recommended to reduce background noise and reverberation.

*   *   *   *

Conference facilities should assist communication   (6-1)

Chapter 6
Meeting and Conference Facilities

Meeting and conference facilities are an important component of many properties. Motor inns typically provide rooms for meetings, civic luncheons, banquets, and receptions. Hotel function space is used for sales and marketing meetings, training programs, seminars, lectures, and workshops. Convention hotels host trade shows and exhibits and resort hotels offer conference facilities. At many properties, meetings and events are also a significant factor in guestroom and food and beverage sales.

The objective of most planned events is the communication and exchange of information. To support this objective, meeting spaces should permit access by all attendees, including those with restricted mobility, and should provide an environment with technical support to aid communication among all participants, including those with sensory impairments.

Conference rooms should include suitable visual aids.   (6-2)

RECEPTION LOBBIES: Reception and registration areas should be connected to the lobby and designated entrances by accessible routes. Permanent or temporary signage should provide guidance and program information in large, clear lettering on a contrasting background color. To fill out registration material, built-in counters or portable tables should provide wheelchair kneespace. Registration areas should include comfortable seats for waiting, convenient to accessible public facilities, such as drinking fountains, telephones, and restrooms.

MEETING and CONFERENCE ROOMS: Meeting, conference, and breakout rooms should be accessible to participants with restricted mobility and include visual aids, lighting, and acoustics to assist individuals with impaired hearing or restricted vision in participating in discussions and presentations.

For access, meeting room doors (or the operable leaf of pairs of doors) should be at least 3'-0" wide, with lever handles and adequate maneuvering clearances. (See Fiugre 3.29.) To minimize interruptions, doors should have high and low peep holes or sidelights with curtains. Meeting rooms should provide clear aisles around the conference table to allow attendees with restricted mobility to move freely to seating locations or the speaking area. This typically requires a clearance of approximately 4'-6" between the edge of the conference table and the surrounding walls or peripheral furniture.

Conference tables should provide kneespace a minimum of 2'-3" high, 1'-7" deep, and 2'-6" wide. To coordinate with the table height, chairs should have a seat height of approximately 18" or should be individually adjustable.

Figure 6.10 Meeting rooms should provide access to seating, speaking and display areas. The lighting and acoustics of the room should aid attendees with restricted vision or impaired hearing.

Chairs should have armrests, low enough to pass below the tabletop so attendees can move close to the writing surface. Seating in conference rooms should offer unobstructed views of the presentation or display area.

Display areas should have directional lighting that can be adjusted from within the room. Windows should have blinds and blackout drapes to control natural light and glare. Marker boards, chalkboards, and fixed microphones should be adjustable in height, so they can be raised or lowered for short speakers or speakers in wheelchairs. Because some participants cannot use podiums, hand-held or lapel microphones should also be available.

The acoustic environment should assist participants in hearing presentations and discussion. Walls, folding partitions, and doors should be sound-insulated for acoustic isolation from adjoining meetings, corridors, and lobbies. Sound-absorbing materials should be used for room finishes and furnishings to reduce reverberation and background noise. Portable listening systems should be available on request.

Seating Capacity	Wheelchair Locations
50 to 75	3
76 to 100	4
101 to 150	5
151 to 200	6
201 to 300	7
301 to 400	8
401 to 500	9

Figure 6.11 UFAS minimums for wheelchair seating spaces. For seating capacities between 500 and 1000, 2% of total and seating is required. Over 1000 seats, 20 seats and an additional seat per 100 over 1000. These are general standards, but specific functions could require more spaces.

A tiered amphitheater with built-in desks   (6-3)

LECTURE ROOMS and AMPHITHEATERS: Conference and convention hotels often provide two types of fixed-seat meeting facilities, lecture rooms with sloping floors and tiered amphitheaters with built-in desks. In either facility, all attendees should be able to participate as either members of the audience or as speakers. This requires accessible seating and accessible routes to entrances, emergency exits, and the speakers' platform. In addition, visual aids and audio-amplification equipment should be provided to assist individuals with restricted vision or impaired hearing.

Wheelchair seating should be dispersed and integrated into the total seating plan, affording comparable sightlines to these attendees. ANSI does not specify the minimum number of wheelchair seating spaces. As a guide, the Uniformed Federal Accessibility Standards for seating are provided in Figure 6.11. Wheelchair spaces should be level, 2'-9" wide by 4'-0" deep if accessible from the front or rear and 5'-0" deep if accessible from side aisles. (See Figure 6.12.)

In theaters or lecture rooms with sloped floors, it is difficult to provide level wheelchair seating and maintain proper sightlines. The seat height of wheelchairs is 1 1/2" to 2 1/2" higher than most theater seating which also affects sight-lines. Unless the room has intermediate cross-rows, the most practical wheelchair seating is in the front and rear cross-rows. The floor is usually level at the front row and wheelchair spaces with front access can be easily pro-vided. However, sightlines of seating directly behind these spaces are slightly compromised. Front cross-rows should be at least 4'-0" wide because wheelchair footrests project 16" into the aisle-width.

To maintain sightlines for the rear row of seating, continu-ous floor slope is necessary. A level wheelchair space in

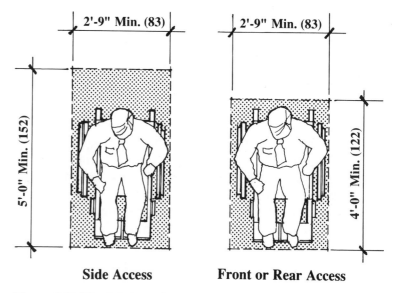

Side Access   **Front or Rear Access**

Figure 6.12 Wheelchair seating should be at level areas 2'-9" wide. Spaces accessed from the front or rear can be 4'-0" deep. Spaces accessed from the side should be 5'-0" deep.

Figure 6.13 Wheelchair seating locations in a lecture room with a sloped floor are only practical in the front and rear rows unless cross rows are provided. Because the wheelchair seat is higher than most theater seating, attendees seated in the rear row have compa-rable sightlines without the floor slope.

Seating areas should be available adjacent to meeting rooms.   (6-4)

the rear row requires a warp in the slab or a small step unless the floor under the rear row is totally level and the seat heights slightly elevated. In level seating areas, sections of fixed seating can be designed for removal to increase wheelchair seating capacity as necessary. (See Figure 6.15.) The higher seat height for fixed seating is also convenient for many older attendees.

Theater seating typically has low, slanted seats, with armrests to help attendees sit and rise. Narrow aisles and fixed armrests, however, can make access to interior seats difficult. Aisles between rows should be at least 1'-6" wide (with seats retracted) for access and legroom. Attendees with leg braces or crutches may be unable to bend their legs and therefore require 18" to 24" of additional legroom. This is typically available in front-row seating unless a modesty screen blocks the leg space.

Aisle seats with swing-up armrests are easier for some guests to access.

Desks in tiered amphitheaters should include a knee-space at least 2'-3" high, 2'-6" wide, and 1'-7" deep for wheelchair access. Desk-tops 2'-4" to 2'-5" high (without aprons) provide writing surfaces that are accessible to guests in wheelchairs and convenient for guests in chairs with a seat height of approximately 18". Raised leaves (see Figure 5.14) can be available for attendees in wheelchairs with high armrests. For short guests, extra cushions and foot platforms can also be provided. Access aisles should be at least 3'-6" wide. Desktops should be no deeper than 2'-0" and lips are helpful to prevent pencils or papers from slipping off the back edge. Individual desk lights aid attendees with restricted vision.

Figure 6.14 With the addition of ramped aisles, tiered amphitheaters can provide wheelchair access to alternating rows. Built-in desks for attendees in wheelchairs should provide adequate kneespace and the aisles should be 3'-6" wide.

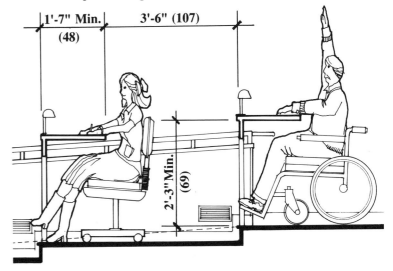

Aisles in tiered amphitheaters or lecture rooms should provide access from the entrances to seating and the speakers' platform. The slope of most lecture halls is approximately 6 1/2 percent, within limits for ramps. If the slope exceeds 5 percent, however, handrails should be provided where side aisles are adjacent to walls. In large rooms with long horizontal-runs, level areas should be provided at appropriate intervals. (See Figure 3.16.) If the slope exceeds 1:12, a separate accessible ramp should connect the rear row with the front cross-aisle.

In tiered amphitheaters, ramped aisles can access alternating rows of seating. (See Figures 6.14 and 6.19.) Handrails should be provided at the ramp-segments and steps. A ramp should also connect the front cross-aisle to the speakers' platform. All aisles and steps should have low-level lighting to aid attendees when the room is darkened for visual presentations.

Figure 6.15 Because of the increased depth for side access, a rear cross-aisle requires little additional space. This aisle allows more flexible wheelchair seating and better egress for all attendees.

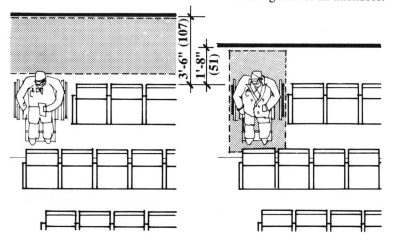

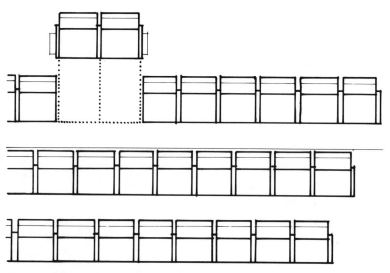

Figure 6.16 Removable sections of seating in level front and rear rows allow the wheelchair seating capacity to be adjusted for individual events. (See photograph, page 148.)

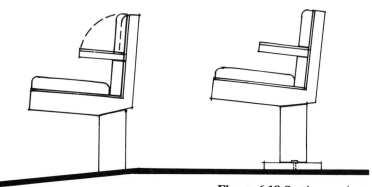

Figure 6. 17 A removable or "swing-away" armrest allows easier access to aisle seating for guests with restricted mobility.

Figure 6.18 Seating sections for level floor areas can be designed for removal when necessary and reinstallation when fixed seats are required.

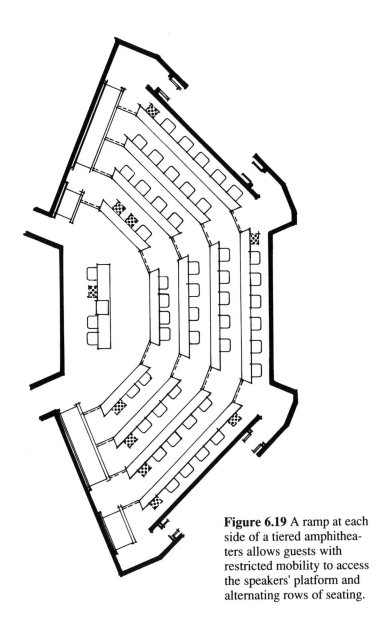

Figure 6.19 A ramp at each side of a tiered amphitheaters allows guests with restricted mobility to access the speakers' platform and alternating rows of seating.

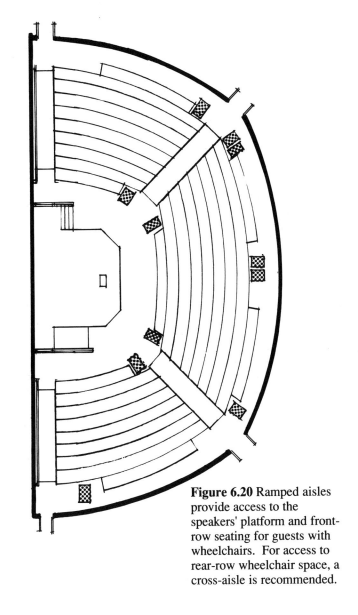

Figure 6.20 Ramped aisles provide access to the speakers' platform and front-row seating for guests with wheelchairs. For access to rear-row wheelchair space, a cross-aisle is recommended.

LISTENING SYSTEMS: Hearing aids are used by many individuals with impaired hearing but are ineffective when guests are distant from the sound source, a high level of background noise is present, or sound echos or reverberates. In lecture halls or amphitheaters, hearing-impaired attendees may be subject to all of these conditions. To overcome this problem, several types of assistive listening systems are available to supplement conventional sound amplification. ANSI permits hardwired earphones with individual volume controls or any of the following systems:

Induction loops are lengths of wire installed around selected seating areas and connected through amplifiers to the speaker's microphone. Within the magnetic field, hearing aids equipped with T-settings (microphone by-pass) receive the transmitted sound. **Wireless FM** listening systems can be used with or without a hearing aid. The sound is picked up by a microphone near the speaker and broadcast by radio waves to headsets, earphones, or hearing aids with T-settings. **Infrared systems** rebroadcast sound in the form of light. The signal is picked up on special receiver headsets that can be used with or without hearing aids.

Listening system headset

For individuals with impaired hearing, observing the gestures and facial expressions of speakers can be critical to understanding the presentation. Therefore, listening systems installed in fixed seating should be located within 50' of the speakers' platform.

Attendees who are deaf require interpreters who communicate the speaker's words using speech-reading or sign language. A small lamp or spotlight should be provided to the side of the speakers' platform to light the interpreter when lecture rooms are dimmed for slide presentations.

Rear projectors make viewing easier and reduce noise level . (6-5)

VISUAL SYSTEMS: Screens for visual presentations, such as slides or videos should be as large as practical. In large meeting rooms, particularly those without sloped floors, overhead television monitors may be used to assist participants seated in rear rows. Built-in front or rear projection rooms eliminate slide or video projectors as obstacles to viewing and as sources of noise.

NOTE: *Recommendations for the number of accessible elements in meeting and conference facilities are provided in Chapter 9, pages 145 and 149.*

Reception Lobbies *(page 104)*

■ The reception area should be connected by an accessible route to the main lobby and/or a separate and accessible entrance and drop-off. *(ANSI 4.3)*

■ Accessible public facilities, such as drinking fountains, telephones, and restrooms, should be convenient to the reception area. *(ANSI 4.1)* Comfortable seating should be available for waiting.

☐ Built-in or portable reception desks should be accessible for guests in wheelchairs. Signage and display boards should be easy to read.

Meeting and Conference Rooms *(pages104 and 105)*

☐ Conference rooms should provide access for participants with restricted mobility to seating locations and the speaking area. The conference table should provide wheelchair kneespace, and the seat height of chairs should be coordinated with the table height.

☐ Portable or built-in audio-visual systems, such as amplification systems and television monitors, should be available for attendees with restricted vision or impaired hearing.

☐ To reduce background noise, meeting room walls should be sound-insulated and finishes and furnishings within the room should use sound-absorbent materials.

☐ Presentation areas in conference rooms should be well-lit and include accessible display boards and microphones.

Lecture Rooms and Amphitheaters *(pages 105 -109)*

■ Accessible seating for attendees in wheelchairs should be provided at dispersed locations, with sightlines comparable to other seats. *(ANSI 4.31.3)*

■ Wheelchair seating spaces should be level areas, 2'-9" wide by 4'-0" deep for front or rear access and 5'-0" deep for side access. *(ANSI 4.31.2)*

■ Desks in amphitheaters should provide sufficient kneespace and footroom. *(ANSI 4.30)* Individual lights are recommended at each seating location.

■ Speakers' platforms should be accessible to speakers with restricted mobility. *(ANSI 4.31.5)*

☐ Theater seating with swing-up armrests are recommended at aisle seats.

Listening Systems *(page 110)*

■ If an audio-amplification system is provided, a listening system, such as induction loops, wireless FM, or infrared systems, to assist persons with severe hearing loss should also be available. *(ANSI 4.31.1)*

■ If a listening system is provided for fixed seats, the seating should be within 50' of the speakers' platform. *(ANSI 4.31.6)*

Visual Systems *(page 110)*

☐ Visual systems, such as large screens or television monitors, should be provided to aid guests with restricted vision.

*   *   *   *

111

Recreational facilities can be beneficial to many guests with physical impairments. (7-1)

Chapter 7
Recreational Facilities

Hotels and motels offer a variety of recreational activities, ranging from swimming pools and health clubs, at small properties, to golf courses, ski complexes, and marinas at resort hotels and conference centers. To increase revenues, many of these recreational facilities are also made available for community use.

Because of the health benefits of recreational facilities, access for people with physical impairments has always been important. Wheelchairs were first used in Bath, England, for access to the hot mineral springs built by the Romans in the first century A.D. Today, wheelchairs in England are often referred to as Bath chairs. In the United States today, 80 percent of vacation travelers are between the ages of 55 and 74. By the year 2000, this age group is expected to increase by 13 percent. Therefore, recreational facilities at hotels and motels should be designed for use by guests with a range of capabilities.

Outdoor dining spaces should also be accessible. (7-2)

Rest areas should include seating, trash receptacles, and, where possible, lighting. Selected rest areas on long walks or trails should include facilities such as drinking fountains, canopies, and restrooms.

Benches at rest areas should have backs and armrests. The bench seat should be 16" to 18" deep and approximately 18" high. The seat should incline slightly to the rear for comfort and to drain rainwater. Benches and trash receptacles should be located at least 1'-0" from the edges of the paved walking surface. A 3'-0"-wide paved clear space is recommended adjacent to benches for wheelchair seating or children's strollers.

Clear directional signage is important for orientation. Signage should be mounted near eye level, approximately 5'-0" above the walk. For night use, the signage and surface of the walk should be lit. (See Walks, Chapter 2.)

OUTDOOR SPACES, WALKS, and REST AREAS: Terraces, gardens, pool decks, game areas, and other outdoor recreation spaces should be designed for the use and enjoyment of guests with restricted capabilities. To help meet this objective, these outdoor spaces should be connected to the hotel or motel by accessible routes.

Rest areas should be provided on long walks that connect elements such as gardens, docks, golf courses, or tennis courts. For guests with restricted mobility or limited stamina, time as well as distance can be a problem. Travel time can be twice that required for other guests, not including periodic rest stops. For these guests, rest stops should be provided at intervals between 100' and 200'.

Rest areas should be located to provide protection from adverse elements and take advantage of site amenities.

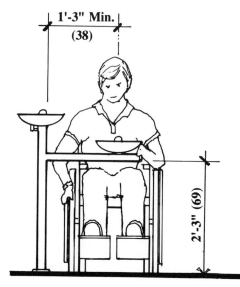

1'-3" Min.
(38)

2'-3" (69)

Figure 7.10 Outdoor drinking fountains should also be accessible to guests in wheelchairs. Hi/low units are recommended. (See Drinking Fountains, page 49.)

Outdoor spaces and recreation areas should offer guests protection from the elements. Accessible restrooms, telephones, drinking fountains, and other public facilities should be available within a convenient travel distance. In hot climates, a portion of the outdoor space should be protected by shade devices such as umbrellas, trellises, or deciduous trees. Walls or trees can provide protection from strong prevailing winds. Remote outdoor spaces or recreation areas should also include canopies or similar protection from sudden rain showers.

Raised planters allow older guests or guests in wheelchairs to see, touch, and smell flowers and low planting. Paving materials for outdoor spaces should meet the requirements for accessible walks described in Chapter 2. Ramps or lifts should be provided at vertical level-changes. Where outdoor dining is provided, aisles, tables, and chairs should meet the requirements in Chapter 5.

Figure 7.11 Benches at rest areas should have backs and armrests and kickspace below. The seat should be approximately 18" above the walk and the armrests 8" above the seat.

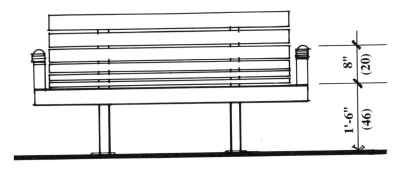

Outdoor spaces should offer protection from the elements.　　(7-3)

115

SWIMMING POOLS: Swimming is an excellent form of recreation and exercise for older guests and guests with restricted mobility because the natural buoyancy provided by water allows more freedom of movement than other forms of exercise. For many guests, entering and exiting the pool are the major obstacles to its enjoyment. Steps or pool ladders can be difficult and hazardous for guests with poor balance and barriers to guests in wheelchairs.

Several alternatives allow guests in wheelchairs to enter and exit the pool, although many, such as raised-edge copings or movable pool floors, are not suitable for hotels or motels. These alternatives require extensive modifications to traditional pool designs and do not address the needs of all guests with restricted mobility.

Lifts to assist guests in wheelchairs can be permanently mounted or portable. Manual, hydraulic, pneumatic, or electric lifts are available. Portable, manually-operated lifts are the least expensive and most flexible alternative. These lifts can be easily removed from cast-in-place anchor sleeves, and stored when not in use. To use a lift, a wheelchair guest slides the sling below his or her body, the pool staff turns the rachet handle to raise the guest clear of the wheelchair, the lift is rotated over the pool, and the guest is lowered into the water. To exit, the guest summons the staff, repositions the sling, and the process is reversed.

Electric or pneumatic lifts can be operated independently, without staff asssistance, but require compressors and permanent electric service at pool side. All lifts are awkward for older guests with poor balance or limited agility, and for safety, the pool staff should be experienced and trained in lift operation. Tiered-platforms are another alter-

A portable, manually-operated lift and sling   (7-4)

native for guests in wheelchairs to independently enter or exit the pool. (See Figure 7.14.)

Ramps into the shallow end of the pool are a safe and convenient alternative if space is available and local building codes permit. Ramps can be used by children, older guests, and guests with restricted mobility. The slope of ramps should not exceed 1:12, and handrails should be provided on both sides. Ramps should have a nonslip, nonabrasive surface and a minimum width of 3'-0". To use the ramp, guests in wheelchairs transfer to a shower chair that can be totally submerged without damage. Clear space in the shallow portion of the pool should be available to temporarily store unattended chairs while guests swim. Where ramps are provided, shower chairs should be available on request.

Steps should also be provided for guests to enter and exit the pool. The handrail configuration should allow a choice of support on the right or left side. This requires either a single handrail in the center of steps 6'-0" or more in width or handrails on both sides. Handrails should continue past the first and last tread. (See Figure 3.19.) Treads should have a nonslip and nonabrasive finish, and the tread width and riser height should meet ANSI requirements. For the safety of swimmers, steps can be located in a recess at the shallow end of the pool. In small pools, underwater benches (See Figure 7.13) can be provided to allow

guests to sit in the water. The edges of all pool construction and equipment should be rounded.

For safety, paving materials surrounding the pool should have a slip-resistant (minimum 0.6 coefficient wet/dry) finish that is not abrasive to bare feet. The edge of the pool can be highlighted by a contrasting color or a change in paving materials. Depth markings should be clearly displayed at the edge of the pool. For safety at night, pools should be lit and capable of being secured after hours of operation.

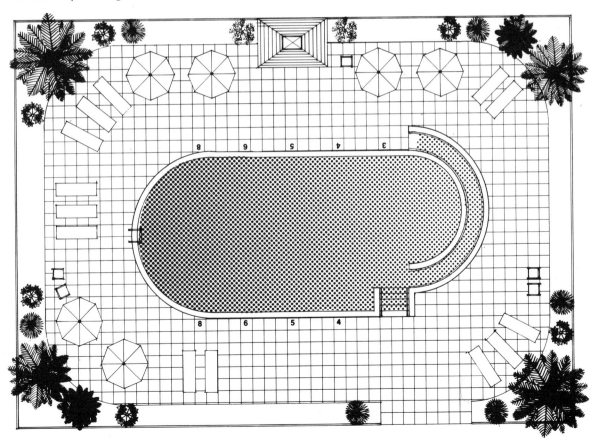

Figure 7.12 If space and codes permit, ramps are a safe and convenient alternative for guests with restricted mobility. The maximum slope of the ramp is 1:12 and handrails should be provided on both sides. Space should be provided for shower chairs to be left unattended at the foot of the ramp while guests swim.

Handrails should be provided at steps into whirlpools. (7-5)

WHIRLPOOLS: Whirlpools are beneficial for many guests, although access can be difficult for guests with restricted mobility or poor balance. Steps, rather than ladders, should be provided to enter the whirlpool. The tread width and riser height should meet ANSI requirements. Handrails should be provided on both sides of the steps and continue 1'-0" past the first and last tread. (See Figure 7.14.) Built-in bench seating in the pool should provide kickspace below the seat to help guests rise. (See Figure 7.13)

For guests in wheelchairs, lifts can be provided for access to whirlpools. To accommodate a lift, a 2'-6" wide section of the bench seat is typically removed in front of the lift. Tiered platforms are an alternative system that allows guests to independently enter a whirlpool or swimming pool. These platforms resemble a small segment of a set of steps. To use a tiered platform, staff should position the

unit in front of the steps. Guests then transfer from the wheelchair seat to the top step and lower themselves, step-by-step, into the whirlpool. Tiered platforms can be filled with water for stability or attached to cast-in anchors for more portable use.

If tiered platforms are provided, the handrails at the steps should have a second low rail at a height of 6" to 12". A clear area 5'-0" wide by 5'-0" deep, should be available at the top of the steps for the wheelchair and platform.

An accessible route, including ramps if necessary, should connect the room entrance to the whirlpool. The floor surrounding the whirlpool should have a slip-resistant and nonabrasive finish. Use of a contrasting color at the coping helps to visually define the edge of the pool.

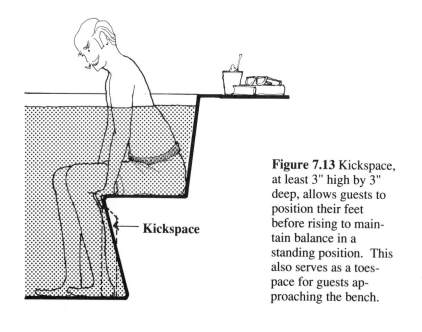

Kickspace

Figure 7.13 Kickspace, at least 3" high by 3" deep, allows guests to position their feet before rising to maintain balance in a standing position. This also serves as a toespace for guests approaching the bench.

118

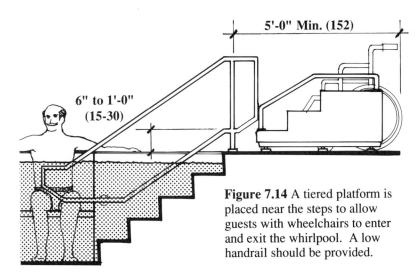

5'-0" Min. (152)

6" to 1'-0" (15-30)

Figure 7.14 A tiered platform is placed near the steps to allow guests with wheelchairs to enter and exit the whirlpool. A low handrail should be provided.

SAUNA ROOMS: The temperature in saunas will heat the metal parts of assistive devices such as wheelchairs, leg braces, canes, or walkers. For safety, staff should remove these devices after guests are seated, which may temporarily leave them immobile until the attendant returns. Because saunas may cause or complicate an incapacitating medical problem, an emergency call system or telephone is recommended.

For guests with restricted mobility, sauna rooms should have doors 3'-0" wide with pull handles of a non-metallic material, and the necessary maneuvering clearances. If the door threshold exceeds 1/2" in height, a portable ramp should be provided. A 5'-0"-diameter turning space, that can include toespace below the benches, is recommended within the sauna. At least one bench seat should be 17" to 19" high and 16" to 18" deep. A horizontal grab bar made of wood or plastic should be provided for at least one seating position adjacent to a wall. For guests who have difficulty rising, vertical grab bars are also recommended.

EXERCISE ROOMS: Properly selected exercise equipment can serve the needs of many guests with limited physical capabilities. Specially designed wheelchair-accessible exercise equipment is also commercially available. For guests with restricted mobility, exercise stations should be connected to the entrance by an accessible route. Guests with wheelchairs generally use equipment designed for developing arms, chest, shoulders, and other upper body muscles. Movable seats can facilitate use of the apparatus by these guests. Exercise equipment should serve guests with a range of strengths and levels of fitness. The weight or resistance of equipment should be adjustable to accommodate individual capabilities. For the safety of all guests, springs, weights, levers, or other moving parts should not cause injury if inadvertently released.

Wheelchair-accessible exercise equipment (7-6)

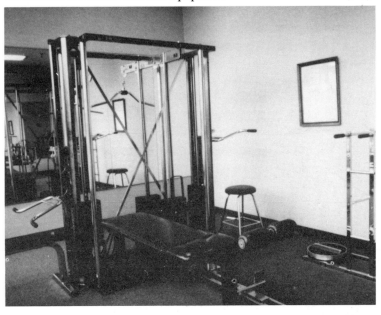

TENNIS, GOLF, and other FACILITIES: Guests of all ages and with varying degrees of physical impairments actively participate in sports and recreation. Athletes in lightweight, maneuverable, high-tech wheelchairs play tennis, racquetball, and basketball. With modified equipment, guests with spinal cord injuries can snow ski, water ski, sail, ride horseback, fish, or scuba dive. Individuals with one arm or leg, as well as guests who are blind, play golf.

Recreational facilities such as tennis courts or golf courses do not require special modifications for accessibility but should be connected by accessible routes to the hotel or motel and associated spaces such as pro shops, snack bars, showers, or locker rooms.

Athletes in wheelchairs participate in many sports.   (7-8)

Active sport facilities should be accessible to guests with a range of capabilities.   (7-7)

LOCKERS and SHOWERS: Locker and shower facilities are often provided in conjunction with recreational activities, such as health clubs, swimming pools, tennis courts, and golf courses and should be accessible. The entrances to locker rooms should include the necessary maneuvering clearances for door operation, particularly when privacy screening or double doors in series are provided. Locker rooms should include accessible lavatories, urinals, and water closets (see Chapter 8) as well as accessible showers, dressing areas, and lockers.

Showers can be accessible in two configurations, stall showers with a built-in seat or roll-in showers, in which guests remain in the wheelchair for showering. However, most guests do not travel with a shower chair, so the stall showers are generally more appropriate. Stall showers should be 3'-0" wide by 3'-0" deep with a curb height of 4" or less. For access, a maneuvering space 3'-0" wide and 4'-0" deep should be provided in front of the stall. The shower should include a bench seat at a height of 18" and grab bars to aid transfer. The shower head should be mounted on an adjustable rod with a 5'-0" hose to allow height adjustment or use as a hand-held spray from a seated position. Temperature controls should be within easy reach from the seat or outside the stall. If a door is provided in lieu of shower curtains, the size and clearances should meet ANSI requirements.

Dressing booths or benches are not appropriate for some guests with restricted mobility who change underclothing in a supine position. For this purpose, a padded platform 2'-

6" deep by 6'-0" long by 18" high should be provided. For transfer, a clear area 4'-0" deep should be provided in front of the platform. Clothes hooks in dressing areas should be installed at a maximum height of 4'-6", and a full-length mirror is recommended. Curtains or a door should be provided for privacy.

For guests with a medical apparatus, privacy for showering and changing is desirable. If space is available, a private area for drying is also recommended. Even with accessible showers and dressing booths, guests often must travel through the more public areas of the locker room while undressed. In larger facilities, or very small facilities, an alternative solution is a private dressing room with a changing platform and an accessible shower, toilet, and lavatory for use by guests of either sex. (See Figure 7.16.)

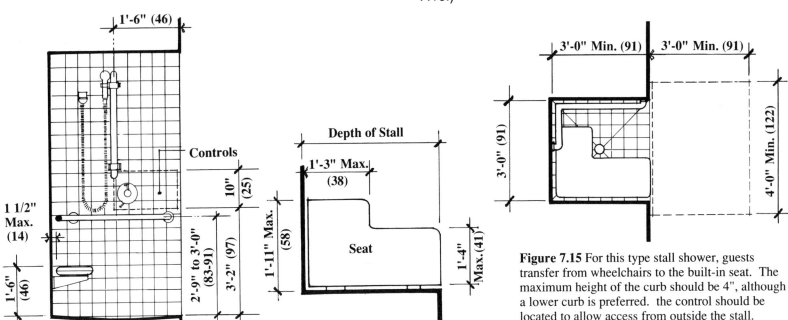

Figure 7.15 For this type stall shower, guests transfer from wheelchairs to the built-in seat. The maximum height of the curb should be 4", although a lower curb is preferred. the control should be located to allow access from outside the stall.

Lockers should also be accessible to guests with re-stricted mobility and unobstructed by fixed benches or equipment. Doors to accessible lockers should provide necessary clearances for operation. Guests with wheel-chairs or walkers usually position themselves parallel to the wall to reach into the locker. Therefore, accessible lockers should be at least 2'-0" from a corner or intersect-ing wall. Clothes hooks in accessible lockers and the top shelf should be no higher than 4'-6". Locker latches and locks should be easy to operate, even for guests with limited hand function or low vision. Latches should allow guests to hook the mechanism to release the catch and open the door with the use of one hand. Built-in combina-tion locks should have large, clear numerals on a contrast-ing background color.

NOTE: *Recommendations for the number of accessible elements in recreational facilities are provided in Chapter 9, page 150.*

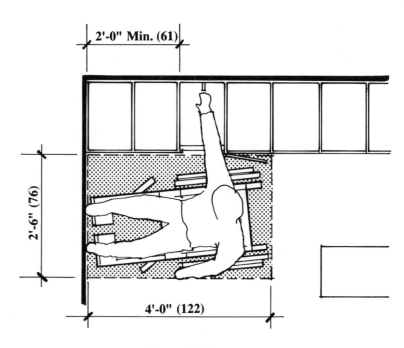

Figure 7.17 To allow parallel wheelchair ap-proach, accessible lockers should be located at least 2'-0" from corners. Access should not be restricted by benches.

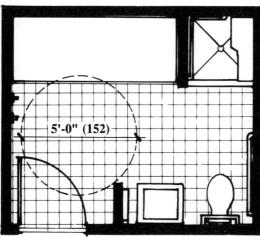

Figure 7.16 A private changing room with a padded platform, and an accessible shower, water closet, and lavatory can be provided for use by guests of either sex.

Outdoor Spaces, Walks & Rest Areas *(pp. 114 -115)*

■ Outdoor terraces, gardens, game areas, and other recreational facilities should be connected to the hotel or motel by accessible routes. *(ANSI 4.1)*

■ Accessible restrooms, phones, and drinking fountains should be provided within a convenient travel distance of remote outdoor facilities. *(ANSI 4.1)*

□ Walks or paths should include rest areas with seating at intervals between 100' and 200'.

□ Benches at rest areas should have backs and armrests, and a seat height of approximately 18". A wheelchair space is recommended adjacent to the bench.

□ Outdoor spaces should include seating areas protected from sun, wind, and rain. Outdoor dining areas should meet the requirements outlined in Chapter 5.

Swimming Pools *(pages 116 and 117))*

■ At least one swimming pool entry and exit alternative should be provided for guests with restricted mobility. *(ANSI 4.1)* A ramp is recommended if building codes permit.

□ Steps into swimming pools should have treads with a slip-resistant finish. The tread width and riser height should meet ANSI standards. Handrails at steps should provide support to the user on the right or left side.

Whirlpools *(page 118)*

■ Whirlpools should include steps with handrails on both sides. *(ANSI 4.1)*

□ One alternative should be provided for guests in wheelchairs to enter. A tiered platform is recommended.

Sauna Rooms *(page 119)*

■ The sauna room door should be 3'-0" wide with handles which are easy to grasp and maneuvering clearances. *(ANSI 4.1)* A 5'-0"-diameter clear turning space is recommended within the sauna.

□ An emergency call system or phone is recommended in sauna rooms.

Exercise Rooms *(page 119)*

■ Exercise rooms should be accessible to guests in wheelchairs. *(ANSI 4.1)*

□ Exercise equipment should be suitable for guests with a range of strengths and fitness.

Tennis, Golf, and other Facilities *(page 120)*

□ Active sports facilities should incorporate accessible routes to the hotel or motel.

Lockers and Showers *(pages 120 and 122)*

■ Entrances and doors to locker rooms should provide necessary clearances for guests with restricted mobility. *(ANSI 4.1)*

■ Locker rooms should include accessible lavatories, urinals, water closets, showers, dressing booths, and lockers as well as provide an accessible route from the entrance to these fixtures.

□ An accessible private changing room is recommended where space permits.

*   *   *   *

Restrooms should include maneuvering space.   (8-1)

Chapter 8
Public Restrooms

Public restrooms should be convenient to all public spaces in hotels and motels, including lobbies, restaurants, bars, lounges, meeting rooms, and recreational areas. Restroom facilities should be connected to these spaces by accessible routes.

ANSI has established two requirements for maneuvering clearances in public restrooms. Restrooms should allow individuals in wheelchairs to enter, close the door, use the fixtures, reopen the door, and exit the room. Restrooms should also include an unobstructed turning space, either a 5'-0"-diameter circle or a "T-shaped" clear area (see Figure 3.26), at one location within the room.

Required clearances for the turning space, door operation, and individual restroom fixtures may overlap. Maneuvering clearances may also include kneespace and toespace below water closets, vanities, and toilet partitions.

Restrooms and fixtures are described in greater detail in the ANSI standard. For further information, refer to ANSI A117.1 or the applicable local code.

Accessible vanity and paper towel dispenser   (8-2)

Vanity tops or the rims of lavatories should be 2'-10" above the floor. This is the maximum height for wheelchair users, and appropriate for most other guests. The vanity top should be shallow, 2'-0" or less in depth, to permit close access to plumbing fixtures and the mirror. Kneespace below the fixture should be 2'-3" high at the apron and bowl and at least 1'-5" deep (see note page 131). Kneespace height may be reduced incrementally as illustrated in Figure 8.11. Kneespace should be at least 2'-6" wide and centered below the basin. Hot water pipes, drain lines, or sharp and abrasive surfaces that abut the kneespace should be insulated or protected. ANSI requires a clear area in front of accessible sinks, 2'-6" wide by 4'-0" deep that may extend up to 1'-7" into the kneespace below the sink.

Basins should be no deeper than 6 1/2". In vanities, oval bowls are recommended to reduce the horizontal-reach to

ENTRY: Accessible restrooms should be identified with a graphic symbol located on the door or an adjacent wall. Restroom doors should be at least 3'-0" wide with hardware that is easy to grasp. Maneuvering room should be provided for door operation, particularly where screen walls are provided for privacy. If doors are equipped with closers, screen walls should be a minimum 4'-6" from the corridor wall. (See Figure 8.10.) Transition-strips between floor finishes should be as flush as possible. Where tile floors are provided, a nonskid finish is recommended.

VANITIES and LAVATORIES: Requirements for vanities and lavatories are similar to those discussed in detail in Accessible Guestrooms, Chapter 4. Briefly restated, these requirements include mounting height, adequate kneespace, and maneuvering room.

Figure 8.10 For doors with closers, a 4'-6" minimum clearance is required between the corridor and screen wall. Even with this clearance, this approach is difficult for guests in wheelchairs, who must push the door past the footrests and turn before the door closes. A 5'-0" clearance is recommended for a conventional approach.

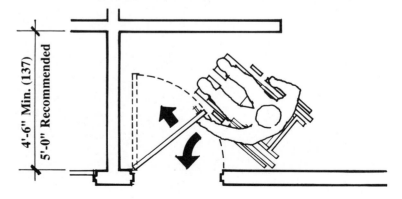

the faucets and controls. Faucets should be easy to grasp and operate. Single-lever controls are recommended. Water temperatures should be clearly indicated with graphics, colors, or symbols. Automatic units should remain open for a minimum of ten seconds.

MIRRORS and ACCESSORIES: Restroom mirrors and accessories should serve all guests. The top edge of the reflecting surface of mirrors should be a minimum of 6'-2" above the floor. For children and guests in wheelchairs, the lower edge should be no higher than 3'-4", although a lower mounting height is preferred. This can be provided even with a 4" splashback above the vanity. A wall-mounted, full-length mirror is also recommended.

Lighting is particularly important at the vanity. The light level does not need to be as high as the guest bathroom

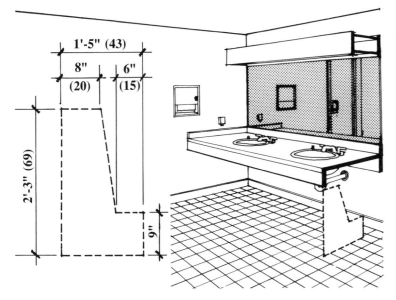

Figure 8.11 The profile of the kneespace below vanities should meet or exceed the requirements illustrated.

but should allow guests to make minor adjustments for grooming or to touch-up makeup (minimum 50 foot-candles recommended). Light at the mirror should be baffled and diffused to reduce glare. The lighting level in other areas of the room should balance the level at the vanity. Light fixtures at toilet stalls should be located to provide appropriate light levels within each stall (minimum 10 footcandles recommended).

Soap dispensers should be mounted within convenient horizontal-reach in locations such as the side wall or vanity top at the rear edge of the bowl. Dispensers should be easy to operate with wet or soapy hands.

Paper towel dispensers should also be within convenient reach, so guests can dry their hands and face while positioned in front of the basin. If a wheelchair must be repositioned to reach the towel dispenser, the guest's wet hands pick up dirt from the chair's rear wheels. Towel advance mechanisms should be simple to operate with one hand and no higher than 4'-6" above the floor. Wall-mounted trash receptacles that project more than 4" from the wall should extend to a minimum height of 2'-3" above the floor.

Hot-air dryers are difficult to locate in close proximity to the basin and, therefore, are not usually recommended. If air dryers are used, they should be mounted in locations that provide an adjacent clear area 2'-6" wide by 4'-0" long. The nozzle should be adjustable and approximately 3'-0" above the floor.

Other accessories such as GFI electrical outlets and paper cup dispensers are also recommended.

TOILET STALLS: At least one toilet stall in each restroom should accommodate guests with restricted mobility. ANSI illustrates four alternatives for accessible toilet stalls that are shown in Figure 8.12. Each stall provides clearances for different maneuvers.

Maneuvering clearances should be provided in accessible stalls for at least one type of wheelchair transfer. There are three methods to approach and transfer from a wheelchair to the seat of the water closet: front transfer, diagonal transfer, and side transfer. (See Figures 4.31 and 4.32.) Side and diagonal transfers are the most commonly used. Many wheelchair users as well as ambulatory guests with walking aids have difficulty maneuvering in narrow stalls. Therefore, standard stalls A and B are strongly recommended. These allow side transfer, diagonal transfer, and use by guests with walkers. Stall A also permits in-swinging doors, so partially open doors to unoccupied stalls are not obstacles to other guests using the facilities. In most restroom configurations, standard stall A can be provided at the end of a row with little or no additional space. (See Figure 8.13.) Alternate stall C accommodates diagonal transfer and walkers, but not side transfer. The smallest stall, alternate stall D, only accommodates front transfer.

Stalls with the minimum dimensions illustrated should have partitions on the front and one side, at least 9" above the

Figure 8.12 ANSI permits several alternative configurations of accessible stalls. The minimum dimensions are predicated on wall-hung water closets and toilet partitions on the entrance side and one side wall at least 9" above the floor.

NOTES: 1. Width should be increased to 4'-0" if approach is from the side or front.
2. Increase 3" if floor mounted water closets are provided.

Standard Stalls (recommended)

Alternate Stalls (not recommended)

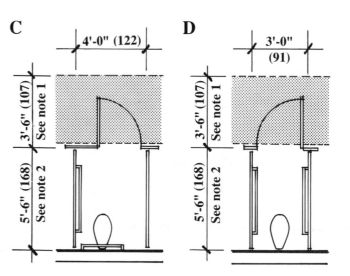

128

floor, to provide sufficient maneuvering clearance. The minimum depth of stalls should be increased 3" if the stall has full-height partitions or less than 9" of toespace. If floor-mounted water closets are provided, the depth of all stalls should be increased 3".

Doors in toilet partitions should provide a 2'-8" clear opening which typically requires a 2'-10" wide door. The arrangement of stall doors should provide maneuvering clearances for the anticipated direction of approach. Door stops projecting from the strike-side of the partition should be rounded to avoid injuries or catching loose clothing. Door latches should be easy to operate, even with poor hand function. Pulls are recommended on both sides of partition doors so that it is not necessary to use the latch

to pull the door closed. Clothes hooks should be mounted no higher than 4'-6" which is near eye level for many guests. Therefore, hooks should be mounted on fixed partitions or carefully located to avoid injuries as the door swings.

Water closets should be mounted with the top of the seat at a height between 17" and 19" (17" recommended). Grab bars should be provided as illustrated in Figure 8.14. to aid balance and transfer. Grab bar anchorage should meet the requirements of ANSI 4.24. Toilet paper dispensers, toilet seat cover dispensers, sanitary napkin disposals, and other accessories should be located within convenient reach of seated guests. Flush controls should be automatic or hand operated, mounted on the widest side of the stall, no higher than 3'-8" above the floor.

Configuration with Stall D
(Not Recommended)   Area: 318 sq. ft.

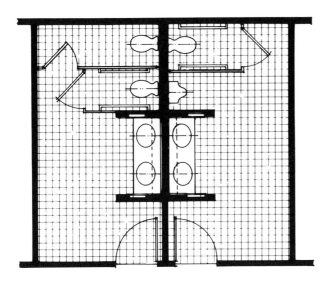

Configuration with Stall A
(Recommended)   Area: 304 sq. ft.

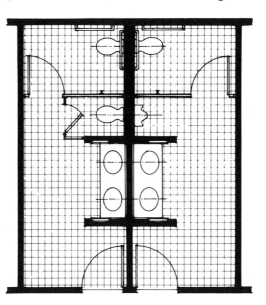

Figure 8.13 Because of the required door clearances for stall D, there is very little space saved in most restroom configurations. Stall A serves more guests, and the door swings into the stall when not in use, eliminating a potential obstacle.

URINALS: Urinals should be either stall-type or wall-hung with an elongated rim projecting at least 1'-2" from the wall. Urinals should be mounted with the rim no higher than 1'-5" above the floor. A clear area 2'-6" wide by 4'-0" long should be provided in front of each accessible urinal. If privacy-screens project beyond the front of the urinal rim, they should be at least 2'-6" apart. Controls for urinals may be automatic or hand operated, and mounted no higher than 3'-8".

NOTE: *Recommendations for the number of accessible elements required in public restrooms are provided in Chapter 9, page 151.*

Grab bars at accessible water closet   (8-3)

Figure 8.14 Ceiling-hung toilet partitions, mounted at least 9" above the floor, increase maneuvering room and also make maintenance easier. Grab bars and accessories should be provided as illustrated.

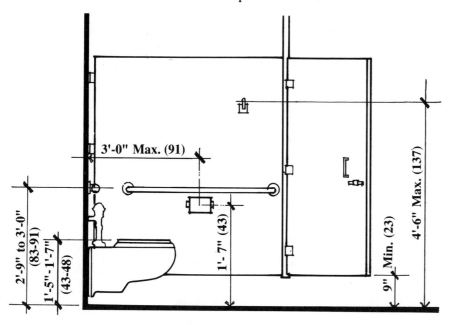

3'-0" Max. (91)

2'-9" to 3'-0" (83-91)

1'-5"-1'-7" (43-48)

1'-7" (43)

9" Min. (23)

4'-6" Max. (137)

Figure 8.15 Urinals should be mounted no higher than 1'-5". Screens that project beyond the rim of the urinal should be at least 2'-6" apart.

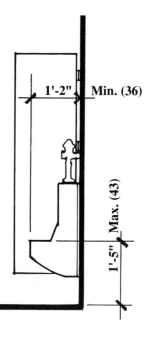

1'-2"   Min. (36)

Max. (43)

1'-5" Max. (43)

Restrooms *(page 125)*

☐ Restrooms should provide maneuvering room to allow guests in wheelchairs to enter, close the door, use the fixtures, reopen the door, and exit. *(ANSI 4.22)*

☐ Restrooms should include an unobstructed turning space, either a 5'-0"-diameter or "T-shaped" clear area. *(ANSI 4.22)*

☐ Accessible fixtures within restrooms should be on accessible routes. *(ANSI 4.17, 4.18, 4.19.)*

Entry *(page 126)*

☐ Restroom doors should be a minimum of 3'-0" wide with easy-to-grasp hardware. Maneuvering space should be provided for door operation. *(ANSI 4.13)*

☐ Accessible restrooms should be identified with the international symbol of accessibility. *(ANSI 4.28.5)*

Vanities and Lavatories *(page 126 and 127)*

☐ The top of vanity counters or lavatories should be no higher than 2'-10" above the floor. Kneespace 2'-5" high*, 1'-5" deep, and 2'-6" wide should be provided directly below the basin. Hot water or drain pipes that abut the kneespace should be protected. *(ANSI 4.19)*

☐ A clear area 2'-6" wide by 4'-0" long should be provided in front of accessible sinks or vanities. *(ANSI 4.19)*

☐ Basins should be no deeper than 6 1/2". Faucets should be easy to operate. Automatic controls should remain open for at least 10 seconds. *(ANSI 4.19)*

* Kneespace at lavatories should be 2'-5" high. As a partial enclosure, a vanity apron can be 2'-3" high.

Mirrors and Accessories *(page 127)*

☐ The lower edge of the reflecting surface of mirrors should be no higher than 3'-4". *(ANSI 4.19)* A lower height is recommended, when possible.

☐ Soap dispensers and paper towel dispensers should be mounted at an accessible height and in convenient and accessible locations. *(ANSI 4.25)*

Toilet Stalls *(pages 128 and 129)*

☐ At least one toilet stall should provide maneuvering clearances for guests with restricted mobility. *(ANSI 4.17)*

☐ Doors in toilet partitions should meet ANSI requirements for width and maneuvering space. *(ANSI 4.17)* Pulls and latches should be easy to grasp and operate.

☐ Water closets should be mounted with the top of the seat between 17" and 19" above the floor. *(ANSI 4.16)* A height of 17" is recommended.

☐ Grab bars, toilet paper dispensers, and other accessories should be provided in accessible stalls as illustrated in Figure 8.14. *(ANSI 4.17)* Anchorage should meet requirements of ANSI 4.24.

Urinals *(page 130)*

☐ Urinals should be stall-type or wall-hung units with the rim no higher than 1'-5". *(ANSI 4.18)*

☐ A clear area 2'-6" by 4'-0" long should be provided in front of accessible urinals. Screens projecting beyond the urinal rim should be at least 2'-6" apart. *(ANSI 4.18)*

*   *   *   *

Planning should anticipate markets years in advance. (9-1)

Chapter 9
Accessible Properties: Scope, Costs, and Recommendations

Each lodging facility is unique in its size, configuration, climate, site topography, and its relationship to other elements of the environment. Each facility offers guests different types of amenities, different levels of service, and charges different rates. The market for each property, is a unique mix of people, traveling for business or pleasure, with different backgrounds, interests, ages, and incomes. The objective of most developers is to earn a reasonable return on their investment. The design of a lodging facility and the resulting construction costs are significant factors in meeting this objective.

Preceding chapters have focused on the design of specific elements that are common to most properties. Which recommendations are most appropriate and cost-effective for a specific project? How many of each accessible feature should be provided? This chapter is intended to help answer these questions.

Chapter 9: Accessible Properties: Scope, Costs and Recommendations

SCOPE: Scope is a term commonly used in building code accessibility provisions to describe the number of accessible elements required in a specific project. For example, how many accessible drinking fountains are required in a hotel? Requirements for scope vary depending on the building code of the local jurisdiction. Most building codes in the United States are based on model codes such as Basic/National Codes (BOCA), or nationally recognized standards, such as ANSI, that are adopted and modified by individual states. Local jurisdictions establish scope requirements for each building occupancy classification. In 1986, ANSI removed scope requirements from A117.1 in an effort to encourage more states to adopt these standards. The Uniform Federal Accessibility Standards (UFAS) contain both design standards and scope requirements for all Federally funded construction.

Scope requirements establish the minimum numbers of accessible elements for a specific project. Owners or developers may elect to exceed the minimum requirements, if in their judgment, increased accessibility will provide greater safety or guest satisfaction. Marketing surveys and other sources of information are usually available to owners or developers to help determine any appropriate increase in the number of accessible elements. In the planning and design of hotels and motels, owners and developers should consider:

1. The number of guests who need or benefit from a specific feature and the consequences to individual guests that result from not providing it.

2. The cost of providing a feature, measured in terms of dollars and increased or decreased convenience to other guests.

A covered loading zone can be a design feature. (9-2)

134

3. The flexibility of adding more accessible elements in the future, if required.

4. Factors unique to the planned property such as the size and configuration of the facility, climate, site topography, or projected market.

Cost is not always a factor. For example, two accessible parking spaces are the same cost as one space. In many cases, accessible features benefit all guests, and the decision to include such features is simply a marketing decision. Each case requires judgment. Therefore, developers and designers are encouraged to examine alternatives, not simply to provide the minimum number of accessible elements.

COSTS: Precise analysis of costs for accessible features cannot be provided in this book because of the range of sizes and finishes in standard designs for lodging facilities. Costs also vary for different functional areas within a property and are affected by the total number of accessible elements constructed. Accessible design features generally have a relatively higher cost in smaller and less expensive properties.

Costs should be measured over the life cycle of either the facility or the individual element. The costs and time periods are a function of complex factors such as the durability of materials, maintenance, and tax depreciation. Approximate first costs of accessible features can be calculated, but changes in the costs of operations or maintenance are more difficult to predict. To determine first costs, accessible features should be measured against costs for standard designs. Premiums for accessible features can be generally categorized as follows:

Accessible features have a relatively low cost in larger properties. (9-3)

1. **Additional space** required for maneuvering clearances in small or restricted spaces

2. **Features** not provided in standard designs or more expensive features substituted for standard features

3. **Portable equipment** provided on request of individual guests

RECOMMENDATIONS and BENEFITS: Summaries of the design recommendations in Chapters 2 through 8 are provided in the following sections with an analysis of guests who benefit from each recommendation. Recommendations which benefit all guests are indicated as secondary benefits. Accessible elements typically subject to scoping provisions are identified and discussed. Relative cost factors are assigned to each recommendation.

CHAPTER 2: Site Access: Most recommended accessible elements provide primary or secondary benefits to many guests with functional impairments. Elements typically subject to scope requirements include:

● **Property entrances** are required by some codes to be connected by accessible routes to public transportation and public walks.
Recommendations: Wherever public walks are located within a reasonable distance of the property, an accessible route should connect the facility to these walks.

● **Passenger loading zones** are typically required at all accessible entrances.
Recommendations: Most secondary building entrances provide fire-egress or greater convenience for guests and staff. Therefore, as many entrances as possible should be accessible and include accessible passenger loading zones. At major entrances, canopies to protect the drop-off area and 8'-6"-wide access aisles are recommended.

● **Parking** spaces are usually required to be a minimum percentage of the total parking and may include one additional space for each accessible guestroom.
Recommendations: Accessible spaces serve guests and staff with restricted mobility or limited strength and stamina. The number of accessible spaces should also reflect associated facilities, such as meeting rooms, restaurants, and recreational activities. Accessible parking should be proportionally distributed to serve all accessible entrances, including separate guest wings and associated facilities.
Costs for accessible parking result from the increased width of access aisles and required curb-ramps. To reduce costs and conserve space, two accessible spaces should share a curb-ramp and access aisle. Therefore,

the number of accessible spaces in a single location is generally a multiple of two. Based on a 9'-0" width for conventional spaces, each pair of accessible spaces is 16 percent wider. Six accessible spaces therefore require a total width equal to seven conventional spaces.

Parking for accessible vans is not addressed by most codes.
Recommendations: Van parking spaces serve guests who use wheelchairs. Because these spaces serve fewer guests, they should be a small percentage of the total accessible spaces. They should be located near the entrance to the registration lobby or accessible guestrooms. Spaces should be reserved by special signage.
Costs can be reduced by using wide walks or two van spaces sharing an 8'-6" access aisle.

● **Walks** are typically required to provide at least one accessible route to connect all accessible elements on a site.
Recommendations: Major routes between elements should be accessible walks. Where this is not the case, signage should be provided to the alternate route.

Recommended portable equipment can include an accessible van for limosine service.
Costs may be partially offset by tax incentives provided under Section 190 of the U.S. Internal Revenue Code.

Figure 9.10 Recommendations for Site Access

Chapter 2: Site Access

ACCESSIBLE ELEMENTS

Benefit legend in cells: P = primary benefit (dark), S = secondary benefit (gray)

Accessible Elements	Hearing	Vision	Tactile Senses	Range-of-Motion	Hand Function	Strength & Stamina	Mobility	Cognitive Abilities	Recommendations	Scope	$
1. PROPERTY ENTRANCE										●	
a. Signage	S	P	S	S	S	S	P	P	Directional signage		-
b. Route *	S	P	S	S	S	S	P	P	Accessible walks at urban sites		+
2. PASSENGER LOADING ZONE										●	
a. Canopy *	S	P	S	P	P	P	P		At major entrances		+
b. Lighting	P	P	S	P	S	P	P	P	Minimum 6 footcandles		-
c. Access aisle *	S	S	S	S	S	S	P	S	Width of 8'-6" at major entrances		-
d. Curb ramp *	S		S	P	P	P	P		Flush-transitions at major entrances		-
e. Benches/Seating	S	S	S	S	S	P	S		Protected by canopy		-
3. PARKING										●	
a. Parking spaces *						P	P		Marked access aisles		+
b. Van parking spaces							P		Minimum width of 16'-6"		+
c. Lighting	P	P	S				P		Minimum 1 footcandle		-
4. DRIVES & CURB-RAMPS											
a. Curbs	S	S	S	P	P	S	S	S	Maximum height of 6"		-
b. Crosswalks	S	P	S	S	S	S	S	S	Visual and tactile markings & lighting		-
c. Signage	S	P	S	S	S	S	S	S	Illuminated directional signage		-
d. Curb-ramps *	S		S	P	P	S	S		Low-level lighting		-
5. WALKS										●	
a. Width & slope *	S	S	S	S	S	S	P	S	Minimum width of 6'-0"		-
b. Materials & colors	S	P	S	S	S	S	P		Highlight edges & interfaces		-
c. Signage	S	P	S	S	S	S	S	S	Illuminated directional signage		-
d. Lighting	P	P	S	S	S	S	P		For safety and security (min. 1 FC)		-
e. Vertical Level-changes *	S	P	S	P	P	P	P		Alternatives to steps or escalators		+
f. Vertical clearances *	S	P	S	S	S	S	P		Minimum of 6'-8"		-
g. Horizontal clearances	S	P	S	S	S	S	P		Landscape & furniture-strips		+
6. DETECTABLE WARNINGS											
a. Warning surfaces *	S	P	S	S	S	S	S	P	Or change in colors & materials		-

Legend: ■ primary benefit ▨ secondary benefit * addressed by ANSI ● subject to scoping (See page 136) + significant cost - nominal cost

CHAPTER 3: Entry, Lobby, and Public Circulation Spaces: Most accessible elements recommended for these spaces offer either primary or secondary benefits to guests with a range of functional impairments at little additional cost. With careful planning, costs associated with elements such as lifts, ramps, or elevators can be minimized. Space for maneuvering clearances is usually available because public areas are relatively large and open. Fire exit requirements for corridor and door widths typically exceed requirements for accessibility. Elements that are typically subject to scoping provisions include:

● **Entrances** are addressed by most codes. At least one principal entrance is typically required to be accessible. For buildings with multiple entrance levels, one entrance at each level may be required to be accessible. Entrances that are part of accessible routes, connecting accessible elements on the site, are also required to be accessible. *Recommendations*: For both convenience and safety, as many entrances as possible should be accessible and exit directly to grade. An overhang should protect accessible entrances. In cold or moderate climates, vestibules are recommended at all entrances serving public spaces.

● **Signage** for emergency information, general circulation, or space identification may be required to meet standards for size, character proportion, and background colors. *Recommendations*: All signage should meet these standards in addition to recommendations for lighting, mounting height, graphic symbols, and tactile lettering.

● **Ramps and level-changes** are often part of accessible routes. Codes typically require a minimum of one accessible route to connect all accessible elements within the property.

As many entrances as possible should be accessible. (9-4)

Recommendations: All major circulation routes to elements providing basic services for guests should be accessible. Whenever practical, these routes should be level, without lifts or ramps. If secondary accessible routes or supplemental elevators are provided, signage at appropriate locations should clearly indicate the alternate route. If long ramps are provided, elevator service should also be available.

● **Stairs** are required by code in multistory buildings. Stairs for egress, or connecting floors not served by elevators, may also be required to meet accessibility standards. *Recommendation*: All stairs or steps should meet ANSI requirements for treads, risers, and handrails.

Close lighting provides a high level of illumination at the shelf.   (9-5)

● **Elevators** for passenger service are typically required to be accessible.
Recommendations: All passenger elevators should meet ANSI requirements.

● **Public telephones**: Most codes require one accessible phone, compatible with hearing aids and equipped with amplifier handsets, on each floor or one such phone in every bank of phones.
Recommendations: In all locations with single phones, the unit should be mounted at an accessible height and equipped with accessible features. Where multiple phones are provided, units at both heights are recommended. At least one house phone should also be accessible, compatible with hearing aids, and equipped with an amplifier handset.

● **Drinking fountains**: Most codes require either a percentage of accessible units, or at locations where a single drinking fountain is provided, that the unit be accessible.
Recommendations: For the convenience of guests who need water to take medication or for specific medical conditions, it is recommended that high/low accessible drinking fountains be provided at all locations within convenient travel distance of public spaces.

● **Retail spaces** are generally required to provide one accessible entrance. Aisles may be required to be accessible routes and sales counters to be 3'-0" in height or lower.
Recommendations: For guests with restricted mobility, the major and most direct entrance should be accessible.

Furniture groupings are not typically addressed by building codes.
Recommendations: Lobby seating should include at least a small percentage of chairs or sofas that are appropriate for guests with a limited range-of-motion and seating with proper lighting for guests with low vision.

Recommended portable equipment should include a Telecommunication Device for the Deaf (TDD) at the registration desk. If a cut-out is not provided at the registration desk, a clipboard should be available to serve as a writing surface for guests in wheelchairs.

Chapter 3: Entry Lobby, & Public Circulation Spaces

ACCESSIBLE ELEMENTS

Legend: █ = primary benefit, ▒ = secondary benefit

Accessible Elements	Hearing	Vision	Tactile Senses	Range-of-Motion	Hand Function	Strength & Stamina	Mobility	Cognitive Abilities	Recommendations	Scope	$
1. ENTRANCES & VESTIBULES										●	
a. Protection	▒	█	▒	█	▒	█	▒	▒	5'-0" beyond entrance		−
b. Lighting	█	█	▒	▒	▒	▒	█	█	Minimum of 5 footcandles		−
c. Door size & clearances ✳	▒	▒	▒	▒	▒	▒	█	▒	Vestibules at public spaces		+
d. Threshold ✳	▒						█	▒	Low as possible		−
2. FRONT DESK											
a. Counter height	▒	█	▒	█	█	▒	▒	▒	Provide alternate heights		−
b. Lighting	█	█	▒	▒	▒	▒	▒	▒	Minimum of 75 footcandles		−
3. SIGNAGE and WARNINGS										●	
a. Location/lighting	▒	█	▒	▒				█	5'-0" mounting height		−
b. Lettering/background ✳	▒	█	▒					█	Light characters/dark background		−
c. Graphic symbols	▒	█	▒					█	In addition to written information		−
d. Tactile lettering ✳		█							Room numbers		−
e. Hazardous areas ✳	▒	█	▒						Tactile warnings		−
4. RAMPS and LEVEL-CHANGES										●	
a. Alternatives to stairs ✳	▒	▒	▒	█	▒	█	█	▒	Basic services located on one level		+
b. Width/slope ✳	▒	▒	▒	▒	▒	█	█	▒	Minimum width of 5'-0" at long ramps		−
c. Horizontal run ✳	▒	▒	▒	▒	▒	█	█	▒	Alternatives at long, steep ramps		−
d. Vertical level changes ✳	▒	█	▒	▒		▒	█	▒	Provide flush-transitions		−
5. STAIRS										●	
a. Risers and treads ✳	▒	█	▒	█	▒	▒		▒	For all stairs		−
b. Color contrast	▒	█	▒	▒	▒	▒		▒	Visual definition		−
c. Lighting	▒	█	▒	█	▒	█		▒	Location of light source		−
6. HANDRAILS											
a. Size and shape ✳	▒	█	▒	█	█	▒	█		Diameter		−
b. Mounting height ✳	▒	█	▒	█	▒	█	█		Vertical height & horizontal clearance		−
c. Low rails				█					For children at appropriate locations		+
d. Intermediate rails	▒	█	▒	█	▒	▒	█	▒	At wide stairs		+

Legend: █ primary benefit   ▒ secondary benefit   ✳ addressed by ANSI   ● subject to scoping (See page 138)   + significant cost   − nominal cost

Figure 9.11 Recommendations for Entry, Lobby, and Public Circulation Spaces

Chapter 3: (con't) ACCESSIBLE ELEMENTS	Hearing	Vision	Tactile Senses	Range-of-Motion	Hand Function	Strength & Stamina	Mobility	Cognitive Abilities	Recommendations	Scope	$
7. ELEVATORS										●	
a. Cab and door size *	▒	▒	▒	■	▒	▒	■	▒	Handrails, floor finishes		-
b. Controls *	■	▒	▒	■	▒	▒	■	▒	Height, tactile numbers		-
8. PUBLIC TELEPHONES										●	
a. Access *	▒	▒	▒	▒	▒	▒	■	▒	Clear space		-
b. Acoustics	■	▒	▒	▒	▒	▒	▒	▒	Locate away from background noise		-
c. Height *	■	▒	▒	■	■	▒	▒	▒	4'-6" max. or mulitple levels		-
d. Amplification/compatibility *	■								Provide TDD at reception desk		-
e. Shelf & lighting	▒	■	▒	■	■	■	■	■	Minimum 75 footcandles		-
9. DRINKING FOUNTAINS										●	
a. Access *	▒	▒	▒	▒	▒	▒	■	▒	Front approach in alcove		-
b. Height *	▒	▒	▒	■	▒	▒	■	▒	Multiple levels & cup dispenser		-
10. LOBBIES and CORRIDORS											
a. Horizontal clearances *	▒	▒	▒	▒	▒	▒	■	▒	Width and turning space		-
b. Furniture groupings	■	▒	▒	■	▒	▒	▒	■	Seating and reading lights		-
c. Acoustics	■	▒	▒	▒	▒	▒	▒	■	Minimize background noise levels		-
d. Lighting	■	■	▒	▒	▒	▒	▒	■	Lighting levels, glare		-
e. Vertical clearances *	▒	■	▒	▒	▒	▒	▒	■	Projections and minimum height		-
f. Floor & wall finishes	▒	■	▒	▒	▒	▒	■	▒	Finishes and patterns		-
11. RETAIL										●	
a. Entrance & aisles *	▒	■	▒	▒	▒	▒	■	▒	Width and clearances		-
b. Display heights & counters	▒	■	▒	■	▒	▒	■	▒	Vertical heights		-
12. ADMINISTRATIVE OFFICES											
a. Doors/openings *	▒	▒	▒	▒	▒	▒	■	▒	Width and clearances		-
b. Corridors *	▒	■	▒	▒	▒	▒	▒	▒	Accessible routes, 5'-0" width		
c. Accessible restrooms *	▒	■	▒	▒	▒	■	▒	▒	Convenient to administrative offices		-
13. VENDING and LAUNDRY											+
a. Access *	▒	▒	▒	▒	▒	▒	■	▒	5'-0"-diameter turning space		-
b. Equipment	▒	■	▒	■	▒	▒	■	▒	Controls and vertical heights		-

Legend: ■ primary benefit   ▒ secondary benefit   * addressed by ANSI   ● subject to scoping (See page 139)   + significant cost   - nominal cost

CHAPTER 4: Accessible Guestrooms: Most accessible elements recommended for guestrooms offer primary or secondary benefits to guests with a range of functional impairments. Costs of recommended and code required elements can be significant or minor, depending on the typical guestroom design. Most codes include scope requirements for:

● **Accessible guestrooms** are typically required to be a minimum percentage of the total number of guestrooms. The basic design requirements are usually focused on the needs of guests in wheelchairs.

Recommendations: There are a range of features that should be provided in accessible guestrooms to assist these guests and guests with other functional impairments. Accessible guestrooms should be located to minimize travel distances to other guest facilities, including parking, and to provide safe egress in the event of an emergency. In low-rise buildings, accessible rooms should be on floors with direct access to grade. A mix of accessible rooms including doubles, singles, and suites is recommended when practical. Suites, intended for business entertaining, should be have accessible entrances and bathrooms.

Costs for accessible guestrooms are most directly affected by area requirements for maneuvering clearances, including:

1. Greater width and clearance at the entrance, closet, and bathroom doors

2. Wider aisles to access the bed, bedside table, dresser, desk, lights, controls, windows, and draperies

3. Maneuvering space in front of the closet, in the sleeping area, and within the bathroom

Patio doors should also be accessible. (9-6)

4. Increased space for access to the water closet, vanity, tub/shower, and bathroom accessories

Additional costs for providing these clearances depends on the standard guestroom design. Most standard designs provide the maximum useful area in as efficient and attractive a configuration as possible. Therefore, the cost of additional area can be significant, since the basic unit is repeated many times.

In properties with a standard structural bay-spacing of 13' or greater, necessary maneuvering clearances can be provided with little compromise in functional efficiency. Figure 9.12 compares a standard design with a 14' bay-spacing and an accessible guestroom of the same size.

The accessible room has the same size bathroom and a slightly smaller sleeping area (-5 percent). As the width of the standard structural bay is increased, the impact of the maneuvering clearances is reduced and functional compromises are minimized.

For properties with smaller guestrooms and standard structural bay-spacings of 12' or less, it is more difficult to provide maneuvering clearances. Figure 9.13 illustrates a standard guestroom with a 12' bay-spacing and an accessible guestroom. Providing clearances in the bathroom results in a significant reduction (-13 percent) in the already restricted sleeping area. This requires that one bed be eliminated from a typical double room.

Most clearances required for accessible guestrooms are also a benefit to guests who do not use wheelchairs. For example, it is difficult for guests with poor balance or low vision to reach across furniture to open drapes. It is awkward for any guest to pass through a narrow door with luggage.

Portable equipment offers flexibility to modify any guestroom to the needs of individual guests, including:

1. Audible/visual warning signals or telephones compatible with hearing aids

2. Television remote controls, closed-caption decoders, visual alarm clocks, bathroom phone extensions, shower seats, shower ramps, spacer rings for toilet seats, blocking to raise beds for lifts, or display plaques on doors or windows.

Figure 9.12 Comparison of a standard hotel guestroom and accessible guestroom.

Figure 9.13 Comparison of a standard motel guestroom and accessible guestroom.

14' Bay Spacing:

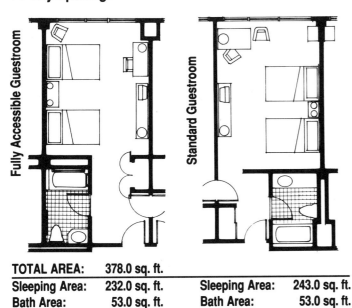

TOTAL AREA:	378.0 sq. ft.		
Sleeping Area:	232.0 sq. ft.	Sleeping Area:	243.0 sq. ft.
Bath Area:	53.0 sq. ft.	Bath Area:	53.0 sq. ft.

12' Bay Spacing:

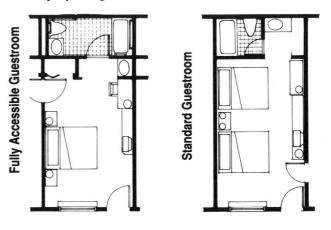

TOTAL AREA:	288.0 sq. ft.		
Sleeping Area:	184.5 sq. ft.	Sleeping Area:	210.5 sq. ft.
Bath Area:	103.5 sq. ft.	Bath Area:	77.5 sq. ft.

143

Chapter 4: Accessible Guestrooms

ACCESSIBLE ELEMENTS	Hearing	Vision	Tactile Senses	Range-of-Motion	Hand Function	Strength & Stamina	Mobility	Cognitive Abilities	Recommendations	Scope	$
1. GUESTROOM ENTRANCE										●	
a. Door clearances/threshold *									Clear area at both strike-side jambs		±
b. Hardware *									Operating controls/heights		−
c. Lighting									Outside each door		±
d. Signage *									Tactile lettering		−
2. CLOSETS											
a. Doors/Access/hardware									Narrow swinging or bifold doors		−
b. Maneuvering space *									5'-0" access aisle		±
c. Rod/shelves *									High/low shelving & rod		−
d. Lighting									For interior of closet		−
3. BEDS											
a. Access									3'-0" access aisle		±
b. Height									18" to 20" high		−
c. Maneuvering space									5'-0"-diameter turning space		+
4. BEDSIDE TABLES											
a. Access									4'-0" aisle or toespace		±
b. Size & height									2" to 3" above mattress		−
5. TELEVISIONS and RADIOS											
a. Remote controls									At bedside table or available		±
b. Screen & height									Large screen, eye level		−
c. Special equipment									Closed-caption decoding available		−
d. Clock radios									Visual signal available on request		−
e. Clock displays and controls									Easy to read and operate		−
6. EMERGENCY WARNINGS											
a. Audible/visual *									Portable or permanent		−
7. GUESTROOM TELEPHONES											
a. Message-flash light									For visual signal and aid to location		−
b. Compatibility *									Use with hearing aids		−
c. Bathroom extension									Location, height, fixed or portable		+

■ primary benefit ▨ secondary benefit * addressed by ANSI ● guestrooms subject to scoping (See page 143) + significant cost − nominal cost

Figure 9.14 Recommendations for Accessible Guestrooms

Chapter 4 (con't)

ACCESSIBLE ELEMENTS

Element	Recommendations	Scope	$
8. LIGHTING and CONTROLS			
a. Switches/controls *	Height, access, operation		-
b. Lamps & reading lights	Location, access, intensity		-
9. FURNITURE and FINISHES			
a. Access/operation/hardware	Height and weight		-
b. Finishes	Materials and colors		-
10. WINDOWS/PATIO DOORS			
a. Windows	Operation and access		-
b. Sliding doors *	Access, size, weight, threshold		-
c. Window treatments	Access to controls		-
11. GUEST BATHROOM			
a. Door & clearances *	In-swinging door, where possible		±
b. Maneuvering space *	5'-0" turning space, where possible		±
12. WATER CLOSETS			
a. Maneuvering space *	Diagonal or side transfer		±
b. Seat height *	17" seat height		-
c. Grab bars *	For transfer and to aid balance		-
13. VANITIES			
a. Height, depth, kneespace *	Narrow top, mitred corner		-
b. Mirror & accessories *	Convenient reach to accessories		-
14. TUBS and SHOWERS			
a. Access *	Full-length access		±
b. Grab bars *	For transfer and to aid balance		-
c. Roll-in showers	Alternative to tub/shower		±
d. Controls *	Access, operation, hot water temp.		-
15. BATHROOM LIGHTING			
a. Lighting levels	Bathroom and vanity		-
b. Finishes & colors	Matte walls, color contrast, nonskid floor		-
16. GRAB BARS/ACCESSORIES			
a. Grab bars, towel bars, etc. *	Height, location, and access		-

Column headers: Hearing, Vision, Tactile Senses, Range-of-Motion, Hand Function, Strength & Stamina, Mobility, Cognitive Abilities

■ primary benefit   ▨ secondary benefit   * addressed by ANSI   ● guestrooms subject to scoping (See page 143)   + significant cost   - nominal cost

CHAPTER 5: Restaurants and Lounges: Most accessible elements recommended offer primary or secondary benefits to guests with a range of functional impairments. Direct costs are not a significant factor, but without careful planning, total seating capacity may be reduced. Elements typically addressed by scoping provisions include:

● **Seating** is only addressed if tables or benches are fixed or built-in. In these instances, codes may require a minimum percentage of accessible seating.
Recommendation: Most restaurants and dining rooms offer customers a choice of seating. A percentage of all seating, whether portable or built-in, should be accessible with similar choices of table size, locations, services, and amenities. Wheelchair-accessible seating should not be grouped at a single table. Therefore to provide 5% accessible seating, for example, a larger (2 to 4 times) percentage of the tables should be accessible.

Some chairs in restaurants and lounges should have an appropriate design and seat height for guests with a limited range-of-motion. Lighting should provide a level of illumination to suit guests with low vision or supplemental lighting should be available.
Costs for accessible furniture should not be higher. Indirect costs can result from a decrease in seating capacity.

Entrances to restaurants or lounges are typically required to include one accessible entrance.
Recommendation: Major entrances should be accessible.

Accessible aisles are typically required to connect accessible elements such as the entrance, accessible seating, self-service areas, and public facilities. However, movable

Lounge seating should offer a range of alternatives for customers. (9-7)

furnishings are not addressed in most codes.
Recommendation: Seating arrangements should include adequate aisle width between tables and chairs and dead-end aisles should provide a 5'-0"-diameter clear area to turn around.

● **Self-service areas** are specified in some codes to have a minimum width and maximum height for tray slides, tableware dispensers and other accessories.
Recommendation: Serving lines should be accessible and include the features described in Chapter 5.

Recommended portable equipment includes portable supplemental lighting, special tableware, portable raised leaves, and braille menus.
Costs for transcribing menus can be offset by using volunteer services in most states.

Figure 9.15 Recommendations for Restaurants and Lounges

Chapter 5: Restaurants and Lounges

ACCESSIBLE ELEMENTS

Legend: **primary benefit** (P), secondary benefit (S), * addressed by ANSI, ● subject to scoping (See page 146), + significant cost, − nominal cost

Accessible Elements	Hearing	Vision	Tactile Senses	Range-of-Motion	Hand Function	Strength & Stamina	Mobility	Cognitive Abilities	Recommendations	Scope	$
1. RESTAURANT SEATING										●	
a. Entrance *	S	P	S	P	S		P	S	Door width and clearances		−
b. Seating for waiting	S	S		S		P	S	S	Comfortable seating in chairs		−
c. Aisles & access	S	P	S	P	S	P	P		Width for passage/access to seating		+
d. Facilies		P	S	S			P		Convenient travel distance		+
2. DINING TABLES & CHAIRS										●	
a. Chair design/seat height	S	S		P		P	S		Armrests, stable, lightweight		−
b. Table, kneespace/footroom*	S			P	S	P	S		2'-5" height, 1'-7" footroom		−
c. Table configuration	P	S					P	S	Narrow width, face-to-face seating		−
3. SELF-SERVICE AREAS										●	
a. Cafeterias	S	P		P	P		P	S	Clearance, display heights, reach		−
b. Salad bars	S	S		P	S	P	P		Plate slides, horizontal reach		−
c. Buffets	S	S		P	S	P	P		Trays, table layout		−
4. TABLEWARE & ACCESSORIES											
a. Utencils & glassware	S	S	S	S	P	S	S		Size, shape, and weight		−
b. Menus	S	P	S					P	Type size & face, color contrast, braille		−
5. LOUNGES & BARS											
a. Entrance *	S	P	S	S	S		P	S	Door width, and clearances		−
b. Aisles *	S	S	S	S	S	S	P		Width for passage/across to seating		+
c. Seating & chairs	S	S		P	S	P	S		Alternatives to low lounge seating		−
d. Bars	S	S		P	P	P	P		When practical, low bar and stools		−
e. Public facilities		P	S	S			P		Convenient travel distance		+
6. LIGHTING											
a. General illumination	P		S	P	P		P	P	Uniform light level, aid mobility		−
b. Task lighting		P	S	S	P	S	S		Adjustable levels		−
7. FINISHES											
a. Floor finishes	S	S		P	S	S	P		Low carpet, secured rugs, nonskid tile		−
b. Acoustics	P	S	S					S	Sound-absorbing finishes		−

■ primary benefit   ▨ secondary benefit   * addressed by ANSI   ● subject to scoping (See page 146)   + significant cost   − nominal cost

CHAPTER 6: Meeting and Conference Facilities: Most recommendations for meeting and conference facilities offer primary and secondary benefits to most guests with functional impairments. Significant cost factors may include wheelchair seating spaces in lecture rooms and ramps in tiered amphitheaters. Many codes include scope requirements for:

● **Reception lobbies,** meeting rooms, lecture rooms, and amphitheaters are usually required to have at least one accessible entrance served by an accessible route. *Recommendation*: For safety, all major entrances and as many other entrances as practical should be accessible.

● **Lecture/amphitheaters** may be required to provide the following accessible elements:

Wheelchair seating is typically specified as a minimum number and/or percentage of total seating. *Recommendations*: Provisions for wheelchair seating should be as flexible as possible in terms of the number of spaces and their location to allow facilities to be adjusted to accommodate specific events that may require significantly higher numbers of spaces. *Costs* for providing additional wheelchair seating capacity can be reduced by using removable seating sections.

Desks in tiered amphitheaters are built-in work surfaces and therefore may be required to provide a minimum percentage of accessible spaces. *Recommendation*: These desks can be designed to make any seating space accessible to guests in wheelchairs with only minor modifications and no additional cost.

Aisles in spaces with fixed seating are addressed in most

Seating can be removed to provide wheelchair spaces. (9-8)

codes. A minimum of one accessible route is usually required to connect accessible elements such as the entrance, seating, speaker's platform, and public facilities. *Recommendation*: Aisles in spaces with portable furnishings should also provide clear access. For safety, as many aisles as practical should be accessible.

Listening systems are also required to provide a minimum percentage or miminum number of portable or built-in amplification systems. *Recommendation*: Portable systems and microphones should be available for all meeting spaces.

Recommended portable equipment for meeting and conference facilities includes portable listening systems, raised leaves to modify desks, hand-held or lapel microphones, and appropriate audio and visual equipment.

Figure 9.16 Recommendations for Meeting and Conference Facilities

Chapter 6: Meeting and Conference Facilities

ACCESSIBLE ELEMENTS

	Hearing	Vision	Tactile Senses	Range of Motion	Hand Function	Strength & Stamina	Mobility	Cognitive Abilities	Recommendations	Scope	$
1. RECEPTION LOBBIES										●	
a. Entrance *	▨	■	▨	■	▨	▨	■	▨	Primary and secondary		−
b. Seating for waiting	▨	■	▨	▨	▨	■	■	▨	Comfortable chairs		−
c. Signage (temporary)	▨	■	▨	▨	▨	▨	▨	■	Type, style, size, & background		−
d. Public facilities *	▨	■	▨	▨	▨	■	■	▨	Convenient to meeting space		±
2. MEETING ROOMS										●	
a. Access *	▨	▨	▨	▨	▨	▨	■	▨	Doors, aisle space		−
b. Seating	▨	▨	▨	■	▨	▨	■	▨	Chair design		−
c. Display area	■	■	▨	▨	▨	▨	■	▨	Lighting, board height, microphones		−
d. Accoustic environment	■	■	▨	▨	▨	▨	▨	▨	Sound insulation, finishes,		−
3. LECTURE/AMPHITHEATERS										●	
a. Access *	▨	■	▨	■	▨	▨	■		Door width and clearances		−
b. Wheelchair seating *							■		Front/rear row, removeable sections		±
c. Theater seating	▨	▨	▨	■	▨	▨	▨		Aisle width, aisle seating		±
d. Desks/chairs *	▨	■	▨	■	▨	▨	▨		Table height, depth, light		−
e. Aisles/ramps *	▨	■	▨	■	▨	▨	■		Width, slope, lighting, railings		±
f. Stage *	■	▨	▨	■	▨	▨	■		Ramp, side light for interpreter		±
4. LISTENING SYSTEMS										●	
a. Portable systems *	■								Induction loops, FM, Infrared		+
5. VISUAL SYSTEMS											
a. Equipment	▨	■	▨	■	▨	▨	▨	▨	Monitors, rear projectors, lg. screens		−

■ primary benefit   ▨ secondary benefit   * addressed by ANSI   ● subject to scoping (See page 148)   + significant cost   − nominal cost

CHAPTER 7: Recreational Facilities: Most accessible elements recommended offer primary or secondary benefits to guests with different types of functional impairments. The most significant cost is construction of a ramp at pools, where this is permitted by codes. Ramps benefit more guests than lifts and are more convenient for guests in wheelchairs. Scope provisions typically address:

● **Recreational facilities** are usually required to be connected by accessible routes to the hotel or motel. En-trances to facilities are typically required to be accessible. *Recommendation*: Accessible routes should be provided to all facilities including those for active sports.

● **Lockers and Showers** are typically required to have accessible entrances and maneuvering space and provide at least one set of accessible fixtures.
Recommendation: Lockers are not addressed by most codes though they are often built-in equipment. A small

Figure 9.17 Recommendations for Recreational Facilities

Chapter 7: Recreational Facilities — ACCESSIBLE ELEMENTS	Hearing	Vision	Tactile Senses	Range-of-Motion	Hand Function	Strength & Stamina	Mobility	Cognitive Abilities	Recommendations	Scope	$
1. **OUTDOOR SPACES**										●	
a. Rest areas									Maximum distance, benches		-
b. Outdoor spaces									Protection, public facilities		+
2. **SWIMMING POOLS**										●	
a. Lifts, ramps, steps									Alternate methods, handrails		+
b. Decks									Surface material, depth markings		-
3. **WHIRLPOOLS**										●	
a. Steps, lifts, platforms									Steps with handrails, tiered platforms		-
4. **SAUNA ROOMS**										●	
a. Access & call system									Clearances, telephone or signal		-
5. **EXERCISE ROOM**										●	
a. Access & equipment									Clearances, range of equipment		
6. **RECREATIONAL FACILITIES**										●	
a. Access & restrooms　*									Accessible route and lockers		+
7. **LOCKERS and SHOWERS**										●	+
a. Showers & dressing　*									Accessible fixtures		+
b. Lockers									Access & controls		-

■ primary benefit　▨ secondary benefit　* addressed by ANSI　● subject to scoping (See text above)　+ significant cost　- nominal cost

percentage of lockers should be accessible to guests with restricted mobility or restricted range-of-motion. If space permits, shower areas should include private drying areas.

Recommended portable equipment should include a lift or tiered platform, if required, to access swimming pools or whirlpools.

CHAPTER 8: Public Restrooms: Most recommendations offer primary benefits to guests with restricted mobility. The design of the vanity, mirror, and lighting, and the location of accessories is also important to other guests. To reduce time and travel distances, accessible restrooms should be convenient to all staff and public spaces. Elements typically addressed by scoping include:

● **Entry** to public restrooms is usually required by codes to be accessible and connected to other common use areas by an accessible route.
Recommendation: Clearances at screen walls should be provided for guests with restricted mobility to enter and exit.

● **Fixtures** are usually required by codes to include one accessible sink or lavatory, mirror, water closet, and urinal.
Recommendation: Accessible water closets should be in standard stalls (see Figure 8.12) whenever possible.

Figure 9.18 Recommendations for Public Restrooms

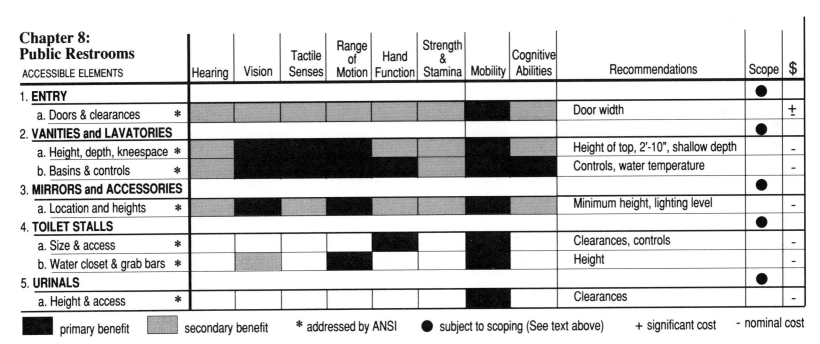

Chapter 8: Public Restrooms ACCESSIBLE ELEMENTS	Hearing	Vision	Tactile Senses	Range of Motion	Hand Function	Strength & Stamina	Mobility	Cognitive Abilities	Recommendations	Scope	$
1. ENTRY										●	
a. Doors & clearances *	░	░	░	░	░	░	█	░	Door width		±
2. VANITIES and LAVATORIES										●	
a. Height, depth, kneespace *	░	█	█	█	░	░	█	░	Height of top, 2'-10", shallow depth		−
b. Basins & controls *	░	█	█	█	█	█	█		Controls, water temperature		−
3. MIRRORS and ACCESSORIES										●	
a. Location and heights *	░	█	░	█	░	░	█	░	Minimum height, lighting level		−
4. TOILET STALLS										●	
a. Size & access *					█		█		Clearances, controls		−
b. Water closet & grab bars *		░		█					Height		−
5. URINALS										●	
a. Height & access *							█		Clearances		−

█ primary benefit	░ secondary benefit	* addressed by ANSI	● subject to scoping (See text above)

+ significant cost   − nominal cost

151

Planning for construction should address the needs of the future. (9-9)

ACCESSIBLE PROPERTIES: The design of hotels and motels must address a wide range of user's needs, from basic protection from the elements and personal security, to more complex requirements such as spatial proportions, transitions, privacy, and separation between activities. Visual images and style are also important. Differences in design reflect the priorities of the designer or the client and compromises are usually necessary, with important objectives taking precedence over lesser considerations. Minimum construction and operating costs, for example, are often important client objectives.

For guests with functional impairments, design elements are usually either assistive, helping or enabling them to perform basic activities or barriers that must be overcome. Barriers usually result from oversight, lack of coordination between disciplines, or other design objectives taking precedence. With a better understanding of their needs, assisting these guests will, hopefully, become a more important design objective.

Guest satisfaction can be increased in every property with more accessible features. The changes are subtle, but they make a difference. Many guests with functional impairments do not actively seek special accommodations and some are reluctant to admit that they have difficulty performing tasks in an environment that appears to meet everone else's needs. Yet, when an assistive environment is provided, the additional hospitality is recognized and appreciated.

Alternatives are available to developers and designers determine both the type and number of accessible elements to provide for a specific project. In public spaces, basic accessibility is required by most building codes. However, additional accessible features are a cost-effective way for a property to provide a more pleasant environment for everyone.

The design of guestrooms is a more complex problem. Properties typically provide a small percentage of accessible guestrooms which are reserved for guests with wheelchairs. Accessible rooms meet code requirements for circulation space and architectural elements such as doors and bathroom fixtures, but may fail to include appropriate furniture arrangements or furnishings. These rooms should be designed and furnished to assist guests with restricted mobility and other guests with a range of functional impairments. How should a property provide accessible features for guests who would not request a "wheelchair" guestroom?

One alternative is to also include accessible features in standard guestrooms such as good reading lights, color-contrast in room finishes, high and low closet shelving, raised shoe shelves, or grab bars in showers. For most properties, these features are a small investment to increase guest satisfaction. Portable equipment to tailor guestrooms to the needs of individual guests is another low-cost alternative.

For properties with larger guestrooms, the maneuvering clearances do not require significant compromises to function or quality of space. At these properties, accessible guestrooms can serve any guest and universal rooms can be a realistic long-term objective.

For smaller guestrooms, typical at properties which provide low-cost lodging, the additional maneuvering clearances require significant compromises in standard guestroom designs. These properties can only realistically provide the required minimum percentage of fully accessible guestrooms. However, even in the smallest rooms, maneuvering clearances can be provided in a functional arrangement that meets the needs of wheelchair users and is also suitable for other guests.

At all properties, basic access should be another consideration in the design of typical guestrooms. While all guestrooms may not provide clearances and features for an overnight stay, a 3'-0"-wide entry door and 2'-8"-wide bathroom door may allow many guests with restricted mobility to access the room for a social visit or business meeting.

Planning for the future is difficult. In this century alone, there have been significant changes in lifestyles, social

Good design withstands the test of time.   (9-10)

patterns, and business practices as well as changes in technologies, such as plumbing and mechanical systems, building materials, and construction techniques. However, the element that has changed the least is typically the user.

Older and historic properties are enjoying a renewed popularity in all parts of the world which reflects an interest in our heritage and an appreciation of their design. Many elements in these buildings show a greater level of concern for the needs of users than buildings constructed in the later part of this century. Covered porches with built-in bench seats, for example, offer protection and comfort while guests wait to be received. Ornate door knockers are not as efficient as electric door bells, but clearly demonstrate concern for visitors who want to make their presence known. Elaborate flared stair bannisters, show the designer's concern for safety. The careful and sensitive design of these structures is admired and appreciated years after construction.

In major renovations of old properties, however, significant retrofit expense is often attributed to false economies at the time of construction. Low floor-to-floor heights in buildings constructed between 1930 and 1955 make retrofitting modern mechanical and air conditioning systems more difficult and expensive than renovations of older buildings with higher ceilings which were originally designed for natural ventilation. The structural bay-spacing in narrow corridors also saved expense in construction, but make it difficult to meet modern fire exit requirements. In many existing structures, a little additional space and expense would have greatly increased the long-term usefulness of the structure.

Demographic changes and advances in medicine are changing the fundamental structure of our society. The built environment will slowly be shaped to reflect these changes. Successful hotel and motel developers use basic formulas for the design and marketing of properties. Prudence dictates that these formulas will change slowly. Hopefully, accessible design will become an important part of the formula as the lodging industry plans for the future. Developers currently planning new hotels or motels have an exciting opportunity to lead the way and make a sound, long-term investment.

Appendices

Appendix A: Information Centers

● National Rehabilitation Information Center (NARIC)
8455 Colesville Road
Suite 935
Silver Spring, MD 20910
(301) 588-9284
(800)34-NARIC

Responds to information requests, prepares a variety of publications, and provides extensive topical research services. Collects and updates fact and referral information regarding practices, programs, and organizations.

Produces two databases: REHABDATA (rahabilitation research) and ABLEDATA (commercially available products). Maintains a library containing hard copy of documents listed on REHABDATA.

● National Information Center on Deafness
Gallaudet University
800 Florida Avenue, NE
Merrill Learning Center, Room LE54
Washington, DC 20002
(202) 651-5051 (Voice/TDD)

Centralized source of information on deafness. Responds to inquiries from parents, professionals, and deaf individuals. Disseminates fact sheets, resource listings, and other materials.

● National Center for Health Statistics
3700 East-WEst Highway
Hyattsville, MD 20782
(301) 436-8500

Data collection, analysis, research, and public inquiries.

● Job Accommodation Network (JAN)
West Virginia University
Allen Hall - Room 809
P.O. Box 1622
Morgantown, WV 26506-6122

A service of the President's Committee on Employment of People with Disabilities and supported by the National Institute of Handicapped Research and the Rehabilitation Services Administration. JAN provides a free information system by and for employers regarding job modification and accommodation. The database includes equipment modifications, site modifications, and redesign of job functions to suit functional limitations.

● National Clearinghouse of Rehabilitation Training Materials (NCRTM)
115 Old USDA Building
Stillwater, OK 74078-0433
(405) 624-7560

Disseminates information on rehabilitation with primary concentration on training materials for use by educators of rehabilitation counselors. Have recently added to their collection materials dealing with special education.

● ODPHP Health Information Clearinghouse (OHIC)
P.O. Box 1133
Washington, DC 20013-1133   Mailing Address Only
(800) 336-4797

1010 Wayne Avenue
Silver Spring, MD 20910
(301) 565-4167

Produces a variety of health-related fact sheets. Responds to information requests. Offers a referral system to the broad spectrum of health-related organizations.

- National Information Center for Handicapped Children and Youth (CICHCY)
7926 Jones Branch Drive
Suite 1100
McLean, VA 22102
(703) 893-6061

Responds to information requests and provides names of local resources. Prepares *News Digest, Transition Summary,* and fact sheets.

- Cancer Information Service
National Cancer Institute
Office of Cancer Communications
Bldg. 31, Room 10A-24
9000 Rockville Pike
Bethesda, MD 20892
(303) 496-5583
(800) 4-CANCER

Disseminates cancer education materials to organizations and health care professionals.

- Educational Resources Information Center (ERIC)
US Department of Education/Office of
Educational Research & Improvement
5500 New Jersey Avenue, NW
Washington, DC 20208
(202) 357-6289 (Management)

Collects and disseminates educational documents to teachers, administrators, researchers, students and other interested persons.

Consists of 16 clearinghouses located across the country, each specializing in a particular subject area related to education.

- Association for Retarded Citizens (ARC) of the US
Bioengineering Program
P.O. box 6109
2501 Avenue J
Arlington, TX 76006
(817) 640-0204

Adapts currently available assistive devices for use by retarded persons. Develops new assistive devices when needed. Consolidates information on the use of technological aids into a technology resource library.

- Stout Vocational Rehabilitation Institute, Materials Development Center (MDC)
University of Wisconsin-Stout
Menomonie, WI 54751
(715) 232-1341

Collects, develops, and disseminates information and material on vocational evaluation and work adjustment.

- Accessibility Resource Center
Paralyzed Veterans of America
Architecture and Barrier Free Design Program
801 18th Street, NW
Washington, DC 20006
(202) 872-1300

Disseminates information on barrier-free design. Responds to information requests.

Appendix B: Metric Conversions

TABLE OF CONVERSION FACTORS TO METRIC (S.I.) UNITS

Physical Quantity	To convert from	to	multiply by
Length	inch	meter	2.54×10^{-2}
	foot	m	3.048×10^{-1}
Area	inch^2	m^2	6.4516×10^{-4}
	foot^2	m^2	9.290×10^{-2}
Volume	inch^3	m^3	1.639×10^{-5}
	foot^3	m^3	2.832×10^{-2}
Temperature	Fahrenheit	Celsius	$t_c = (^tF-32)/1.8$
Temperature difference	Fahrenheit	Kelvin	$K = (\Delta^tF)/1.8$
Pressure	inch Hg (60F)	newton/m^2	3.377×10^3
Mass	lbm	kg	4.536×10^{-1}
Mass/unit area	lbm/ft^2	kg/m^2	4.882
Moisture content rate	lbm/ft^2 week	kg/m^{2}s	8.073×10^{-6}
Density	lbm/ft^3	kg/m^3	1.602×10^1
Thermal conductivity	Btu/hr ft^2 (F/inch)	$\dfrac{W}{mK}$	1.442×10^{-1}
U-value	Btu/hr ft^2 F	$\dfrac{W}{m^2K}$	5.678
Thermal resistance	F/(Btu/hr ft^2)	K/(W/m^2)	1.761×10^{-1}
Heat flow	Btu/hr ft^2	W/m^2	3.155

AN INTERPRETATION OF

ANSI A117.1 (1986)
The American National Standard for Buildings and Facilities - Providing Accessibility and Usability for Physically Handicapped People

as applicable to

NEW HOTELS AND MOTELS

by

The American Hotel and Motel Association
Executive Engineers Committee

produced by
The American Hotel and Motel Association
Technology and Information Department
February 3, 1987
888 Seventh Avenue
New York, N.Y. 10106
(212) 265-4506

Appendix C: AH&MA Interpretive Guide

NOTE:

This document is in no way considered to be a standard, binding on any member of the association or industry. Standards, codes and regulations are the exclusive domain of local building and fire code enforcement authorities. **Any question of compliance with regulations should be referred to the building code regulating authority in the locality of construction.**

Introduction

In an attempt to provide clarification of technical information about how to design and construct hotels and motels for improved accessibility by elderly and physically handicapped persons[1], the Executive Engineers Committee of the American Hotel and Motel Association has developed the following interpretive document.

The committee hopes that this document will be of assistance in developing new hotels or motels in compliance with the intent of accessibility regulations while maintaining efficient, safe, attractive and comfortable facilities for all guests.

This is an information document suggesting a level of accessibility consistent with *ANSI A117.1 (1986) American National Standard for Buildings and Facilities - Providing Accessibility and Usability for Physically Handicapped People* and is premised on the philosophy that public spaces should generally be accessible to all guests.

Where making all spaces or elements[2] completely accessible would be undesirable, we recommend that the following percentages found in the *U.S. Uniform Federal Accessibility Standards* for "Acceptable Number of Accessible Elements" be used.

# of Elements	Accessible Elements
1 - 25	1
26 - 50	2
51 - 75	3
76 - 100	4
101 - 150	5
151 - 200	6
201 - 300	7
301 - 400	8
401 - 500	9
501 - 1000	2% of total
1001 and over	20 plus 1 for each 100 over 1000

Acceptable Number of Accessible Elements
from
U.S. Uniform Federal Accessibility Standards

---

[1]physically handicapped person - an individual who has a physical impairment, including impaired sensory, manual, or speaking abilities, that results in a functional limitation in gaining access to and using a building or facility.

[2]element - an architectural or mechanical component of a building, facility, space, or site that can be used in making functional spaces accessible (for example: telephone, curb ramp, door, drinking fountain, seating, water closet).

How To Use This Document

This document is intended to be used in conjunction with ANSI A117.1 (1986) American National Standard for Buildings and Facilities - Providing Accessibility and Usability for Physically Handicapped People.

It is recommended that the user obtain a copy of ANSI A117.1 (1986) from:

Sales Department
The American National Standards Institute
1430 Broadway Avenue
New York, N.Y. 10018

The format of this document is made up of three columns.

1) The first column is a complete reproduction of the ANSI A117.1 (1986) table of contents. It lists all of the criteria found in the ANSI Standard, in the order and with the numbering system of ANSI A117.1 (1986). The use should reference the ANSI Standard for particulars contained under these criteria.

2) The second column provides interpretive comments generated by the Executive Engineers Committee of the American hotel and Motel Association. These comments are intended to illuminate the intent of the ANSI criteria as it affects hotel and motel properties.

3) The third column is a listing of the following seven areas of a hotel or motel which may be affected by the ANSI criteria found in column one. If any of these areas are affected by the ANSI criteria, it has been indicated by an "X" in the appropriate space.

The seven areas of consideration are:

A.	Exterior and Parking
B.	Lobby and Registration Areas
C.	Public Rest Rooms
D.	Restaurants, Bars, and Lounges
E.	Meeting Rooms
F.	Guest Rooms
G.	Health and Recreation Facilities

AH&MA Interpretive Guide (con't)

ANSI Criteria	Interpretive Comments	Exterior & Parking	Lobby and Registration Areas	Public Rest Rooms	Restaurant, Bars, and Lounges	Meeting Rooms	Guest Rooms	Health & Recreation Facilities
1. Purpose and Application		X	X	X	X	X	X	X
1.1 Purpose	This document is intended to assist hotel and motel designers, owners, and developers in creating facilities that are accessible to and usable by physically handicapped (including sensory impaired) and elderly guests. It is, furthermore, intended to assist those guests in allowing them to expect a certain degree of accessibility in new facilities throughout the lodging industry.							
1.2 Application	Newly Constructed Hotels and Motels only.	X	X	X	X	X	X	X
2. Recommendation to Adopting Authorities 2.1 Administration								
2.2 Number of spaces and elements	All public areas of hotels and motels should be made accessible according to the criteria set forth in this document. Accessible guest rooms should be provided according to the ratios shown in the following table of Acceptable Numbers of Accessible Elements found in the US Uniform Federal Accessibility Standard. `# of Elements` `Accessible elements` 1 - 25 1 26 - 50 2 51 - 75 3 76 - 100 4 101 - 150 5 151 - 200 6 201 - 300 7 301 - 400 8 401 - 500 9 501 - 1000 2% of Total 1001 and over 20 plus 1 for each 100 over 1000	X	X	X	X	X	X	X
2.3 Remodeling	The criteria in this document are not intended to cover anything other than the new construction of hotels and motels.							
2.4 Designing for children 2.5 Review procedures								
3. Graphics, Dimensions, Referenced Standards and Definitions								
3.1 Graphic Convention Definitions 3.2 Dimensions 3.3 Referenced American National Standards 3.4 General Terminology 3.5 Definitions								

ANSI Criteria	Interpretive Comments	Exterior & Parking	Lobby and Registration Areas	Public Rest Rooms	Restaurant, Bars, and Lounges	Meeting Rooms	Guest Rooms	Health & Recreation Facilities
4. Accessible elements and spaces		X	X	X	X	X	X	X
4.1 Basic components		X	X	X	X	X	X	X
4.2 Space Allowances and Reach Ranges	A guest in a wheelchair should be able to access all features in accessible guest rooms, as well as any special features such as health equipment, steam baths, or any other special elements provided for guests of the property.	X	X	X	X	X	X	X
4.2.1 Wheelchair Passage Width		X	X	X	X	X	X	X
4.2.2 Width for Wheelchair Passing		X	X	X	X	X	X	X
4.2.3 Wheelchair Turning Space		X	X	X	X	X	X	X
4.2.4 Clear Floor or Ground Space for Wheelchairs	In guest rooms, maneuvering space for guests who use wheelchairs should be provided on at least one side of each bed. Consideration should be given in the layout of the room and its furnishings to facilitate convenient access between and maneuvering space around the telephone, bed and bathroom.\n\nIt is recommended that standard open-legged bed supports be installed in accessible rooms. Enclosed platforms under beds make it impossible for portable lifts to safely lift people to and from the bed.\n\nAccessible maneuvering space should be provided to and around accessible elements in locker rooms, including: lockers, toilets, showers, and equipment.	X	X	X	X	X	X	X
4.2.5 Forward Reach		X	X	X	X	X	X	X
4.2.6 Side Reach		X	X	X	X	X	X	X
4.3 Accessible Route		X	X	X	X	X	X	X
4.3.1 General		X	X	X	X	X	X	X
4.3.2 Location		X	X	X	X	X	X	X
4.3.3 Width		X	X	X	X	X	X	X
4.3.4 Passing Space		X	X	X	X	X	X	X
4.3.5 Headroom		X	X	X	X	X	X	X
4.3.6 Surface texture		X	X	X	X	X	X	X
4.3.7 Slope		X	X	X	X	X	X	X
4.3.8 Changes in level		X	X	X	X	X	X	X
4.3.9 Doors		X	X	X	X	X	X	X
4.3.10 Egress		X	X	X	X	X	X	X
4.4 Protruding objects		X	X	X	X	X	X	X
4.4.1 General		X	X	X	X	X	X	X
4.4.2 Headroom		X	X	X	X	X	X	X
4.5 Ground and Floor Surfaces		X	X	X	X	X	X	X
4.5.1 General		X	X	X	X	X	X	X
4.5.2 Changes in Level		X	X	X	X	X	X	X
4.5.3 Carpet		X	X	X	X	X	X	X
4.5.4 Gratings		X						X
4.6 Parking Spaces and Passenger Loading Zones		X						

Appendix C: AH&MA Interpretive Guide

AH&MA Interpretive Guide (con't)

ANSI Criteria	Interpretive Comments	Exterior & Parking	Lobby and Registration Areas	Public Rest Rooms	Restaurant, Bars, and Lounges	Meeting Rooms	Guest Rooms	Health & Recreation Facilities
4.6.1 General		X						
4.6.2 Parking Spaces		X						
4.6.3 Passenger Loading Zones	The drop-off point at hotel and motel entrances should have a level or gently ramped (1:20 slope or less) surface with a surface texture and a contrasting color so that mobility impaired people will have no difficulty crossing the interface and visually impaired people will have no difficulty recognizing that they are at a vehicular interface.	X						
4.7 Curb Ramps		X						
4.7.1 Location		X						
4.7.2 Slope		X						
4.7.3 Width		X						
4.7.4 Surface		X						
4.7.5 Sides of Curb-Ramps		X						
4.7.6 Built-up Curb-Ramps		X						
4.7.7 Warning textures		X						
4.7.8 Obstructions		X						
4.7.9 Location at Marked Crossings		X						
4.7.10 Diagonal Curb-Ramps		X						
4.7.11 Islands		X						
4.7.12 Uncurbed intersections		X						

ANSI Criteria	Interpretive Comments	Exterior & Parking	Lobby and Registration Areas	Public Rest Rooms	Restaurant, Bars, and Lounges	Meeting Rooms	Guest Rooms	Health & Recreation Facilities
4.8 Ramps	At least one form of accessible access other than stairs should be provided into every swimming pool, whirlpool, or other multiple person bathing tank. Examples of acceptable alternatives include ramps, lifts, transfer tiers, and raised pool edge copings.	X	X	X	X	X	X	X

Ramps used to provide access for disabled people to swimming pools should comply with the criteria found in this section.

Fixed or movable raised transfer platforms with tiers (as illustrated below) may be considered to be one acceptable means of providing access to swimming pools for mobility impaired people.

STEPS WITH RAISED PLATFORM

Raised pool edge copings with appropriate access space and grab bars (as illustrated below) should be considered to be one acceptable means of providing pool access for mobility impaired people.

RAISED POOL EDGE COPING

AH&MA Interpretive Guide (con't)

ANSI Criteria	Interpretive Comments	Exterior & Parking	Lobby and Registration Areas	Public Rest Rooms	Restaurant, Bars, and Lounges	Meeting Rooms	Guest Rooms	Health & Recreation Facilities
4.8.1 General		X	X	X	X	X	X	X
4.8.2 Slope and Rise		X	X	X	X	X	X	X
4.8.3 Clear Width		X	X	X	X	X	X	X
4.8.4 Landings		X	X	X	X	X	X	X
4.8.5 Handrails		X	X	X	X	X	X	X
4.8.6 Cross Slopes and Surfaces		X	X	X	X	X	X	X
4.8.7 Edge Protections		X	X	X	X	X	X	X
4.8.8 Outdoor Conditions		X						X
4.9 Stairs	At least one form of accessible access other than stairs should be provided into every swimming pool, whirpool, or other multiple person bathing tank. Examples of acceptable alternatives include ramps, lifts, transfer tiers, and raised pool edge copings (see "Ramps" above). If stairs are installed in swimming pools, they should comply with the ANSI criteria.	X	X	X	X	X	X	X
4.9.1 General		X	X	X	X	X	X	X
4.9.2 Treads and Risers		X	X	X	X	X	X	X
4.9.3 Nosings		X	X	X	X	X	X	X
4.9.4 Handrails		X	X	X	X	X	X	X
4.10 Elevators								
4.10.1 General								
4.10.2 Automatic Operations								
4.10.3 Hall Call Buttons								
4.10.4 Hall Lanterns								
4.10.5 Raised Characters on Hoistway Entrances								
4.10.6 Door Protective and Reopening device								
4.10.7 Door and Signal Timing for Hall Calls								
4.10.8 Door Delay for Car Calls								
4.10.9 Floor Plan of Elevator Cars								
4.10.10 Floor Surfaces								
4.10.11 Illumination Levels								
4.10.12 Car Controls								
4.10.13 Car Position Indicators								
4.10.14 Emergency Communications								
4.11 Platform lifts		X	X		X	X		X
4.11.1 General		X	X		X	X		X
4.11.2 Requirements		X	X		X	X		X
4.12 Windows	If windows in non-accessible guest rooms are operable, then the windows in the accessible guest rooms should conform to the criteria in this section.						X	

ANSI Criteria	Interpretive Comments	Exterior & Parking	Lobby and Registration Areas	Public Rest Rooms	Restaurant, Bars, and Lounges	Meeting Rooms	Guest Rooms	Health & Recreation Facilities
4.12.1 General							X	
4.12.2 Window hardware							X	
4.13 Doors		X	X	X	X	X	X	X
4.13.1 General	All doors within accessible guest rooms or suites should comply with all ANSI door requirements. (It is recommended that all other guest room entry doors be at least 2'-8" wide and all other guest room, bathroom, and connecting doors be at least 2'-6" wide.)	X	X	X	X	X	X	X
4.13.2 Revolving Doors and Turnstiles			X		X			X
4.13.3 Gates		X			X			X
4.13.4 Double-leaf doorways			X		X	X	X	X
4.13.5 Clear Width		X	X	X	X	X	X	X
4.13.6 Maneuvering Clearances at Doors		X	X	X	X	X	X	X
4.13.7 Two doors in Series		X	X	X	X	X		X
4.13.8 Thresholds at Doorways		X	X	X	X	X		X
4.13.9 Door Hardware	Guest room entry door key or locking device should facilitate operation by someone with arthritic hands or poor hand dexterity. In health facilities or other special purpose areas, locker and other door hardware should comply with the criteria in this section.	X	X	X	X	X	X	X
4.13.10 Door Closers		X	X	X	X	X	X	X
4.13.11 Door Opening Force		X	X	X	X	X	X	X
4.13.12 Automatic Doors			X	X	X	X		X
4.13.13 Power-Assisted Doors and Low Energy Power-Operated Doors			X	X	X	X		X
4.14 Entrances		X	X		X	X	X	X
4.14.1 General		X	X		X	X	X	X
4.14.2 Service Entrances		X	X		X	X		X
4.15 Drinking Fountains and Water Coolers		X				X		X
4.15.1 General		X				X		X
4.15.2 Spout Height		X				X		X
4.15.3 Spout Location		X				X		X
4.15.4 Controls		X				X		X
4.15.5 Clearances		X				X		X
4.16 Water closets			X				X	X
4.16.1 General	The criteria in this section should be used in the design of all toilets in accessible guest rooms and accessible toilets in public and health facility toilet rooms.		X				X	X
4.16.2 Clear Floor Space				X			X	X
4.16.3 Height				X			X	X
4.16.4 Grab Bars				X			X	X

AH&MA Interpretive Guide (con't)

ANSI Criteria	Interpretive Comments	Exterior & Parking	Lobby and Registration Areas	Public Rest Rooms	Restaurant, Bars, and Lounges	Meeting Rooms	Guest Rooms	Health & Recreation Facilities
4.16.5 Flush Controls			X				X	X
4.16.6 Dispensers			X				X	X
4.17 Toilet stalls				X				X
4.17.1 General	The criteria in this section should be used for the design of accessible toilet stalls in all public and health facility toilet rooms.			X				X
4.17.2 Water Closets				X				X
4.17.3 Size and Arrangement				X				X
4.17.4 Toe Clearance				X				X
4.17.5 Doors				X				X
4.17.6 Grab Bars				X				X
4.18 Urinals				X				X
4.18.1 General	The criteria in this section should be applied to the design of urinals in public restrooms and health facility toilet rooms.			X				X
4.18.2 Height				X				X
4.18.3 Clear Floor Space				X				X
4.18.4 Flush Controls				X				X
4.19 Lavatories, Sinks, and Mirrors				X			X	X
4.19.1 General				X			X	X
4.19.2 Height and Clearances				X			X	X
4.19.3 Clear Floor Space				X			X	X
4.19.4 Exposed Pipes and Surfaces				X			X	X
4.19.5 Faucets				X			X	X
4.19.6 Mirrors	A full length mirror in the immediate vicinity of the lavatory meets the intent of the 40" mirror bottom height requirement.			X			X	X
4.20 Bathtubs							X	X
4.20.1 General	Bathtubs in accessible guest rooms and tubs in health facilities should be designed in accordance with this section.						X	X
4.20.2 Floor Space								
4.20.3 Seat								
4.20.4 Grab Bars								
4.20.5 Controls								
4.20.6 Shower Unit								
4.20.7 Bathtub Enclosures								
4.21 Shower Stalls								
4.21.1 General	Showers in accessible guest rooms should be designed in accordance with the criteria in this section.							
4.21.2 Size and Clearances							X	X
4.21.3 Seat							X	X
4.21.4 Grab Bars							X	X
4.21.5 Controls							X	X
4.21.6 Shower Unit							X	X
4.21.7 Curbs							X	X

ANSI Criteria	Interpretive Comments	Exterior & Parking	Lobby and Registration Areas	Public Rest Rooms	Restaurant, Bars, and Lounges	Meeting Rooms	Guest Rooms	Health & Recreation Facilities
4.21.8 Shower Enclosures							X	X
4.22 Toilet Rooms, Bathrooms, Bathing Facilities and Shower Rooms	The criteria of this section covers accessible areas in hotels and motels such as shower rooms, saunas, steambaths, exercise rooms, and locker rooms.							X
4.22.1 General								X
4.22.2 Doors								X
4.22.3 Clear Floor Space								X
4.22.4 Controls and dispensers	In hot areas such as saunas or steambaths, wood or plastic rather than metal control operators should be provided for comfort and safety.							X
4.22.5 Medicine cabinets								X
4.23 Storage							X	
4.23.1 General							X	
4.23.2 Clear Floor Space							X	
4.23.3 Height							X	
4.23.4 Hardware							X	
4.24 Grab Bars, Tub and Shower Seats				X			X	X
4.24.1 General				X			X	X
4.24.2 Size and Spacing of Grab Bars				X			X	X
4.24.3 Structural Strength				X			X	X
4.24.4 Eliminating Hazards				X			X	X
4.25 Controls and Operating Mechanisms		X	X	X	X	X	X	X
4.25.1 General	In accessible guest rooms, all guest room controls, including, but not limited to, thermostat, lights, TV, etc. should be accessible according to the ANSI criteria. In accessible guest rooms, electrical switches or remote control equipment controlling the power to the television and room lights should be located at the head of the bed so that a guest may control those devices without getting out of bed. Closed captioned television decoding equipment should be available upon request at the front desk for guests requiring such equipment.						X	
4.25.2 Clear floor space 4.25.3 Height	(It is recommended that all light switches be located 4'-0" above the floor.) Note: Some codes may restrict control heights. Check with local enforcement authorities.	X X	X X	X X	X X	X X	X X	X X
4.25.4 Operation		X	X	X	X	X	X	X
4.26 Alarms			X	X	X	X	X	X
4.26.1 General			X	X	X	X	X	X
4.26.2 Audible Alarms			X	X	X	X	X	X
4.26.3 Visual Alarms			X	X	X	X	X	X
4.26.4 Auxillary Alarms	A visual alarm device with battery back-up for hearing impaired guests should be available upon request.						X	

AH&MA Interpretive Guide (con't)

ANSI Criteria	Interpretive Comments	Exterior & Parking	Lobby and Registration Areas	Public Rest Rooms	Restaurant, Bars, and Lounges	Meeting Rooms	Guest Rooms	Health & Recreation Facilities
4.27 Detectable Warnings		X	X		X	X		X
4.27.1 General		X	X		X	X		X
4.27.2 Detectable Warnings on Walking Surfaces		X	X		X	X		X
4.27.3 Tactile Warnings on Doors to Hazardous Areas		X	X		X	X		X
4.27.4 Detectable Warnings at Stairs		X	X		X	X		X
4.27.5 Detectable Warnings at Hazardous Vehicular Areas		X						
4.27.6 Detectable Warnings at Reflecting Pools		X						X
4.27.7 Standardization		X	X		X	X	X	X
4.28 Signage		X	X	X	X	X	X	X
4.28.1 General	Guest rooms should be provided with tactile room numbers at 5'-0" above the floor. (See section 4.10.5)	X	X	X	X	X	X	X
4.28.2 Character Proportion		X	X	X	X	X	X	X
4.28.3 Color Contrast		X	X	X	X	X	X	X
4.28.4 Tactile Characters or Symbols		X	X	X	X	X	X	X
4.28.5 Symbols of Accessibility		X	X	X	X	X	X	X
4.29 Telephones		X	X		X	X	X	X
4.29.1 General	Telephones in guest rooms should be located so that they are easily reachable from the bed and from an accessible route of travel in the guest room.	X	X		X	X	X	X
4.29.2 Protruding Objects		X	X		X	X	X	X
4.29.3 Equipment for the Hearing Impaired	All telephones should be compatible with hearing aids for guests with hearing impairments.	X	X		X	X	X	X
4.29.4 Controls		X	X		X	X	X	X
4.29.5 Telephone Directories		X	X		X	X	X	X
4.29.6 Cord Length		X	X		X	X	X	X
4.30 Seating, Tables, and Work Surfaces	The criteria in this section pertains especially to public service areas such as the registration, cashier, concierge, and any other service desk areas in the hotel.		X		X	X	X	X
4.30.1 General	At least one location offering each service should be provided in an accessible manner as indicated by the criteria of this section. A portable clip board or writing surface is an acceptable alternative.		X		X	X	X	X

ANSI Criteria	Interpretive Comments	Exterior & Parking	Lobby and Registration Areas	Public Rest Rooms	Restaurant, Bars, and Lounges	Meeting Rooms	Guest Rooms	Health & Recreation Facilities

4.30.2 Seating	Accessible table seating in restaurants, cafeterias, lounges, bars, etc. should be provided in accordance with the following table which is identical to the table of Acceptable Numbers of Accessible Elements found in the US Uniform Federal Accessibility Standard. (Note: This table is identical to the table shown in section 2.2.)
	
	    # of Elements Accessible elements
	      1 - 25 1
	     26 - 50 2
	     51 - 75 3
	     76 - 100 4
	    101 - 150 5
	    151 - 200 6
	    201 - 300 7
	    301 - 400 8
	    401 - 500 9
	    501 - 1000 2% of Total
	    1001 and over 20 plus 1 for each 100 over 1000
		X			X	X	X	X

4.30.3 Knee Clearances 4.30.4 Height of Work Surfaces		X X			X X	X X	X X	X X
4.31 Auditorium and Assembly Areas 4.31.1 General 4.31.2 Size of Wheelchair Locations 4.31.3 Placement of Wheelchair Locations 4.31.4 Surfaces						X X X X X		
4.31.5 Access to Performing Areas	Removable ramps at a slope no greater than 1:12 are an acceptable alternative means of access to a temporary platform or other temporarily raised area as long as such ramps are available upon short notice for no additional charge. Microphones capable of being relocated for use by a speaker who uses a wheelchair should be provided.					X		
4.31.6 Placement of Listening Systems 4.31.7 Types of Listening Systems						X X		

Appendix C: AH&MA Interpretive Guide

AH&MA Interpretive Guide (con't)

ANSI Criteria	Interpretive Comments	Exterior & Parking	Lobby and Registration Areas	Public Rest Rooms	Restaurant, Bars, and Lounges	Meeting Rooms	Guest Rooms	Health & Recreation Facilities
4.32 Dwelling Units	Criteria for the design of accessible dwelling units are not to be considered appropriate criteria for the design of typical guest rooms, as the intent of the ANSI regulations is for dwelling units to be used by non-transient occupants. The transient nature of hotel and motel guests would make the adaptability features that are the basis of this section unfeasible.							
4.32.1 General 4.32.2 Adaptability 4.32.3 Basic Components 4.32.4 Bathrooms								
4.32.5 Kitchens	If kitchens are provided in accessible guest rooms, they should conform to the criteria in this section.						X	
4.32.6 Laundry Facilities								

Selected Bibliography

American National Standard for building and facilities: Providing Accessibility and Usability for Physically Handicapped People. American National Standards Institute, Inc., 1986.

Barrier-free Environments, ed. Michael J. Bednar. Dowden, Hutchinson & Ross, Inc., 1977.

Barrier Free Exterior Design: Anyone Can Go Anywhere, ed. Gary O. Robinette. Van Nostrand Reinhold Co., 1985.

Boettidor Raschiko, Bettyann. *Housing Interiors for the Disabled and Elderly*. Van Nostrand Reinhold Company, 1982.

Current Population Reports: Household Economic Studies, Disability, Functional Limitations, and Health Insurance Coverage: 1984/85. Bureau of the Census and US Department of Commerce, 1986.

Design for Aging: An Architect's Guide. The American Institute of Architects (AIA) Foundation, 1985.

Digest of Data on Persons with Disabilities. Mathematical Policy Research, Inc., 1984.

Harkness, Sarah P. and James N. Groom, Jr. *Building without Barriers for the Disabled*. Whitney Library of Design, 1976.

Kellogg Smith, Fran, and Fred J. Bertolone, *Bringing Interiors to Light: The Principles and Practices of Lighting Design*. Whitney Library of Design, 1986.

Rubin, Arthur I., and Jacqueline Elder. *Building for People: Behavioral Research Approaches and Direction.* US Department of Commerce, National Bureau of Standards, 1980.

Rutes, Walter A., and Richard H. Penner. *Hotel Planning and Design.* Whitney Library of Design, 1985.

Steinfeld, Edward, et al..*Access to the Built Environment: A Review of Literature.* Department of Architecture, State University of New York. US Government Printing Office, 1979.

Uniform Federal Accessibility Standards. General Services Administration. US Government Printing Office, 1984

List of Figures

List of Photographs

List of Photographs

Index

Index